A Tenderfoot in Colorado

R. B. Townshend

Foreword by
Thomas J. Noel

University Press of Colorado

© 2008 by the University Press of Colorado

Published by the University Press of Colorado
5589 Arapahoe Avenue, Suite 206C
Boulder, Colorado 80303

Previously published by the University of Oklahoma Press

AAUP The University Press of Colorado is a proud member of
the Association of American University Presses.

The University Press of Colorado is a cooperative publishing enterprise
supported, in part, by Adams State College, Colorado State University, Fort
Lewis College, Mesa State College, Metropolitan State College of Denver,
University of Colorado, University of Northern Colorado, and Western State
College of Colorado.

∞ The paper used in this publication meets the minimum requirements of
the American National Standard for Information Sciences—Permanence of
Paper for Printed Library Materials. ANSI Z39.48-1992

Library of Congress Cataloging-in-Publication Data

Townshend, R. B. (Richard Baxter), 1846–1923.
  A tenderfoot in Colorado / by R.B. Townshend ; with an introduction by
Thomas J. Noel.
    p. cm. – (Timberline books)
  Originally published: [New ed.] Norman : University of Oklahoma Press,
[1968].
  ISBN 978-0-87081-938-4 (pbk. : alk. paper) 1. Colorado—Description and
travel. 2. Rocky Mountains—Description and travel. 3. Townshend, R. B.
(Richard Baxter), 1846–1923—Travel—Colorado. 4. Pioneers—Colorado—
Biography. 5. English—Colorado—Biography. 6. Frontier and pioneer
life—Colorado. 7. Colorado—History—To 1876. I. Title.
  F780.T69 2008
  978.8'02092—dc22
  [B]

                                                                  2008038596

Cover design by Daniel Pratt

CONTENTS

FOREWORD

Welcome to this nugget of Western history, which takes you back to Colorado Territory in 1869 to watch Ute warriors in action, brawls with desperados, buffalo hunts, and longhorn cattle drives from Texas to Colorado.

A Tenderfoot in Colorado is the first reprint in the University Press of Colorado's Timberline Series. With this series we hope to introduce readers to both the best new research on the Highest State and also out-of-print Colorado classics. This work by Richard Baxter Townshend belongs on the shelf beside better-known books by other British observers of Western America, such as William A. Bell, Isabella Bird, Lord Dunraven, Rudyard Kipling, Robert Lewis Stevenson, and Oscar Wilde.

Townshend (1846–1923) was born into a well-heeled English family where his oldest brother was slated to inherit the family land. Giving him further reason to leave home, the young man suffered terrible headaches after falling from his horse. Colorado's curative climate, about which he had learned from the books of Samuel Bowles, attracted him. He arrived in

Cheyenne, Wyoming Territory, in 1869, fresh from Cambridge University, where he had studied classical literature, Latin, and French. A slender lad with long curly hair, bright blue eyes, and pink cheeks, he looked every part the tenderfoot as he stepped off the Union Pacific Railroad. He then boarded Wells Fargo's four-horse stage, heading south to Denver City and life in Colorado Territory "on the ragged edge." On that edge, the tenderfoot would become a superb marksman, horseman, cattleman, and observer. He also would learn how to stalk an antelope, capture a wild longhorn, and cook cattle-drive beans.

Townshend and a partner established a cattle ranch along Black Squirrel Creek on the Arkansas (south) slope of the Palmer Divide in El Paso County. To the west, Pikes Peak shone through the "incredible transparency" of Colorado's dry, crystalline air. At that mountain's base, he witnessed Colorado Springs grow into a town and fill with so many Britons that it was dubbed "Little London." Townshend reported that the town "was run by a very tony company, on teetotal lines, and any man there who wanted a drink had to go a couple of miles around the end of the mesa to Colorado City, or Old Town as it was called, where he could find a saloon" (p. 187).

Colorado Springs may have been dry in booze, but Denver City was drying up in population. In 1867, it had been eclipsed by Cheyenne when the transcontinental railroad bypassed the Colorado Rockies for the gentler hills of Wyoming. Townshend observed in 1869 that

"[n]obody seemed to be very prosperous in Denver just then; indeed the capital city of the Territory had only about 5,000 inhabitants and seemed to be a bit down on its luck" (p. 44). In the territory's northeast corner, Julesburg consisted "of about three and a half dilapidated board shanties stuck down on a treeless waste of yellowish-brown buffalo grass . . . prairie littered for miles with old tin cans and empty bottles" (p. 2). Central City was also struggling, with "many mining-shafts closed and stamp mills idle . . . waiting for the railway to come and wake things up" (p. 47).

Colorado's boom and bust nature is laid bare in *Tenderfoot.* In 1870, only a year after finding the capital a dwindling town, Townshend watched as the Denver Pacific Railway snorted into town, saving the city with a rail lifeline. He found some Denverites celebrating and described the scene:

> [In] a bar-room . . . some men with whiskey bottles and glasses set out before them sang out to me: "Come 'n hev' a drink."
>
> "No, thank you," I replied without pulling up. In a moment out flashed a revolver pointed start at my head.
>
> "Yes, you will," said the same voice with emphasis, "or else—"
>
> What "else" meant was left to the imagination, but I didn't find it hard to guess. My reply was: "Oh certainly," and I sprang from my saddle, saying, "I'd rather drink than be shot any day." (p. 109)

The tenderfoot met Colorado's first territorial governor William Gilpin, who he described as "brainy" and commented that he "writes even loftier than he speaks" (p. 41). He wrote that Gilpin "received me cordially, shook hands, and at once began to hold forth" on Colorado's status as the Garden of Eden, the promised land where "the highest amplitude and altitude of the continent is attained" (p. 55). Townshend cattily noted that Gilpin—the great visionary, developer, and owner of a million acres—was forced to use a friend's office because he apparently could not afford his own.

Townshend focused a sharp eye—and ear—on the pioneers. He witnessed a fundamentalist preacher baptize hundreds by total immersion in a South Platte River ditch (probably Denver's City Ditch) while explaining that those murky waters could wash away all sins. At the Twenty Mile House, the stage stop and tavern that eventually became Parker, Colorado, he watched a "gut-shot" cowboy undergo surgery on the front bar. The "surgeon" used whiskey as the only anesthesia and employed a barber's razor to slice into the patient. No sooner was the cowboy relieved of the bullet than Tiger Bill, slouched in a corner of the bar, woke up from a drunken stupor to threaten the life of tavern keeper Corny Dowd: "There came a flash of petticoats," Townshend described next, "and Mrs. Dowd . . . darted into the bar with a feminine screech and set her ten commandments in his face, dragging her nails down each cheek" (p. 63).

Tiger Bill is the first of many desperados to bloody these pages. Along with Billy the Kid, Wild Bill, and Liver-eating Johnson, there is no shortage of rustlers, crooked gamblers, and gunmen. "Everybody in North America," Townshend speculated, "was born, so to speak, with a gun in his hand and a six-shooter in his hip pocket" (p. 258).

Townshend reported on Indian wars, graphically describing Ute Indian rituals, including how the women mourned horribly for their husbands fallen in battle. His descriptions create beautiful images, as in the following about the Los Pinos reservation:

> [I]n a lovely natural park on the Gunnison [River], the first frosts had painted yellow and scarlet the quakenasp [aspen trees] and dwarf oak. . . . The cone-shaped teepes of the Utes stood in clusters, each band grouped, as its sub-chief chose, near wood and water. Naked Indian boys were driving wiry ponies back and forth through the grass, and other boys were coming up from the creek with strings of splendid trout, and the gaily-dressed bucks rode in from the hills with dripping red lumps of fresh-killed venison and elk-meat hanging to their saddles. (p. 97)

Townshend also described ugly scenes of environmental devastation. He found once-clear streams and the trout in them choked by sawdust from massive tree cutting. Amid many mutilated tree stumps, boomtowns rose with raw, yellow skeleton buildings of unseasoned boards. Seeing how palefaces had ravished

the land, he sympathized with the growing hostility of
the Utes as he reported a Ute attack:

> They dashed fully eight hundred strong from the
> timber[,] . . . their gleaming guns in their hands,
> their faces black with war-paint, their naked
> bronze bodies shining in the bright sun, the
> feathers in their long hair dancing behind them
> in the breeze. Shawano [Shavano] himself in all
> his glory led them, his gorgeous war-bonnet of
> eagle-plumes streaming out four feet behind him.
> To right, to left, he circled in swinging curves,
> the endless line of warriors following him; then
> as if by magic he sent separate bands flying this
> way and that, forwards and backwards, weaving
> a maze of figures like a dance. And every man of
> the eight hundred as he raced along seemed to be
> part of his pony . . . (p. 100)

Among the tenderfoot's adventures the most dangerous was a serious injury from the kick of a half-
broken mare. It happened while he was alone in the
wilds where wolves, coyotes, and crows closed in
to finish him off. Scared that he might be captured
and tortured by Indians, he saved his last bullet for
himself.

Townshend was rescued by a fellow cowhand and
returned to his ranch. There he watched Brigham
Young, as the biggest bulls were commonly named,
successfully fight rivals to establish dominance over
the herd. Longhorn bulls, he noted, were shot by lo-
cals trying to improve their herds with beefier short-

horns. Townshend recorded that South Park's Sam
Hartzel pioneered better breeding when he bought a
$1,000 shorthorn Hereford bull to upgrade his and his
neighbors' livestock.

Townshend's love of animals shines throughout
this book, especially in his tale of rescuing an aban-
doned calf. In another chapter, he bemoaned the dis-
appearance of pronghorn after a market meat hunter
killed 300 with a high-powered telescope rifle in only
three weeks. The buffalo, not the grizzly bear, according to Townshend, was the king of Colorado beasts.
In a tribute to the bison that once dominated the High
Plains he included a memorable story of an old defeated bull isolated from his herd. Alone, stiff, and
weak from past battles and a nasty red gash left by a
rival's horns, the solitary old bull faced his last fight
as hungry wolves smelled his blood and closed in for
the kill.

As a linguist, Townshend collected slang phrases
like "you bet your boots," "a jumping-off-place" (i.e., a
lynching), "tin-horn," and "mushroom city." He cor-
rectly used a tilde in "Cañon City" and called the territory's residents "Coloradans," not the incorrect but
widely used "Coloradoans." He also traced ranching
terms to their Spanish origins.

Townshend marveled at the wealthy "lungers"
with tuberculosis who were replacing the pioneers.
He watched the rise of Colorado's women's suffrage
movement—which in 1893 made Colorado the first
state where men voted directly to fully enfranchise

women. Twenty-three years before that vote, the tenderfoot overheard a woman complain: "I won't obey any laws I don't help to make! It's an abominable shame, the men make the laws, or wretches who call themselves men, execute them and give poor women no chance" (p. 248).

Although exhibiting some of the anti-Mormon and anti-Semitic language common in those days, Townshend was surprisingly tolerant of Mexicans. He described Mexican cowboys as "courteous, high-spirited, courageous," and superior to "young Anglo-Saxon cowboys" (p. 267). At his ranch he hired Hispanic ranch hands, paid them a generous $40 a month, and later called them his partners when he sold his ranch in Colorado and headed to New Mexico in 1874 to try sheepherding, about which he wrote in *A Tenderfoot in New Mexico*.

Eventually, Townshend returned to England to become an eccentric scholar at Oxford, where he entertained faculty and students with his roping, riding, shooting, and tale telling. He translated Latin into English for Clarendon Press and served as treasurer of the Oxford University Golf Club. He also performed in musicals where his remarkable ability to alter his pitch led his friend Sir Edward William Elgar, the composer of *Pomp and Circumstance*, to mimic Townshend in his *Enigma Variations*.

This expert horseman spent his last days riding a tricycle equipped with a little bell to warn others of his approach. In 1899 he published his first book, the

novel *White Pine*, which was followed by *Bullwhack Joe. A Tenderfoot in Colorado* (originally published by London's John Lane Bodley Head Limited) was published three years before his death in 1926, followed by *Last Memories of a Tenderfoot* (London, 1926). We hope you will enjoy this revival of *A Tenderfoot in Colorado* and agree that it is a candid, entertaining, and unusually insightful look at Colorado's territorial times.

—THOMAS J. NOEL,
CO-EDITOR, TIMBERLINE SERIES

A Tenderfoot
in Colorado

A TENDERFOOT IN COLORADO

CHAPTER I

ENTER THE TENDERFOOT

IN 1869 I found myself five thousand miles to the westward of Old England, in a car on the newly opened Union Pacific Railroad, with a good hope of being safely landed by it in the part of the Far West known as Wyoming Territory, U.S.A. I was a tenderfoot, though the title itself was strange to me ; but I was out to learn, and when I heard the strange word used by a man near me on the car I turned to my neighbour, a friendly Westerner with whom I had had lots of conversation since we left Omaha, Neb., and asked :

" What on earth does he mean by a tenderfoot ? "

He looked at me with a smile, saw his chance, and started to spread himself.

" It began like this," he explained. " Some ten or eleven years back, when they first struck gold in Gregory Gulch, and every soul who could started to get to Pike's Peak, or bust, a good five hundred miles across the Great Plains, there was lots of fellers that jes' hoofed it on their ten toes the whole blessed road. You can bet their feet

1

was pretty well skinned for them by the time they got to Pike's Peak, and naturally the other fellers who'd been before 'em and got healed up first set themselves up for real old-timers, and took the notion of calling every new arrival a tenderfoot."

" Oh," said I, " then it just means a new-comer, pure and simple! "

" Pure ! " he fairly laughed aloud. " Well, I don't know so much about ' pure,' but ' simple ' wouldn't be so far out mostly. The simple tenderfoot don't know the ropes, and you bet he's got lots to learn."

" I suppose that means, then "—I hesitated— "that—that I'm a tenderfoot ? "

" Why, certainly ! " He smiled back at me. " And if you'll not be offended by my saying so, you look it all over."

" Offended ?   Me ?   Not in the least. Why should I be ? "   Had I not only just ceased to be an undergraduate at Trinity, Cambridge, rejoicing there in the title of Cherub, though I can't say whether it was my blue eyes and curly hair, or my pink cheeks and innocent expression that earned me the name in college.

" Julesburg ! " shouted the conductor—*anglice* guard—putting his head in at the end door of the car. " Any here for Julesburg ? "

Nobody was for Julesburg and, looking out of the window, I couldn't feel surprised there should be nobody, for the town seemed to consist of about three and a half dilapidated board shanties stuck down in a treeless waste of yellowish-brown buffalo

grass, which spread on every side to the horizon, in wide rolling downs.

"Not much of a place now," commented my companion, whom by the way, I had learned to call Mr. Crocker, "but when I was travelling this route about two years back Julesburg was a pretty lively hole. 'Hell on wheels,' they called it. It was the end of the railroad track already laid, and the beginning of the new grade under construction where the company had thousands of hands at work. Every month these chaps, when they got their money, used to come in here to Julesburg to spree it off. There's a few of their relics over yonder."

Our train was already moving out of the depot (station), and the prairie was littered for miles with old tin cans and empty bottles. Also, on the outskirts of what had once been the town, there stood almost a forest of little wooden crosses sticking up at all sorts of angles, survivors of more that had fallen down.

"You can bet there's a few pretty hard citizens planted under there," said Mr. Crocker. "They didn't call this place 'Hell on wheels' for nothing. Why, Julesburg thought nothing of having a man for breakfast ; and quite often they used to have two or three."

A man for breakfast ! "Well," I thought, "I may be a tenderfoot, but I'm not going to give myself away to Crocker by inquiring if he means to imply that Julesburg was addicted to cannibalism. Of course he's only indulging in American humour.' A fortnight spent in New York and

Boston had enlightened me as far as that. Nevertheless, Mr. Crocker spotted by my eye that he had puzzled me.

" A man for breakfast means that somebody's got slugged overnight in one of the dives around town, or bin shot in the lay-out of some tin-horn," he explained. But to me this explanation was hardly more lucid than the puzzle. Pretty obviously, Mr. Crocker was talking the language of the Far West for my special benefit, and what a " dive " might be, I could perhaps guess, but " the lay-out of a tin-horn " was still too much for me. However, what had I come to the Far West for but to learn ? " What's a lay-out ? and what's a tin-horn ? " I ventured.

" A tin-horn's a gambler. That is," he corrected his definition, " it means a special type of gambler, and a low-down one at that. Some gamblers are quite ' way-up ' men of course."

It was not hard to guess " way-up," so I held my tongue without inquiring. Mr. Crocker looked at me critically as he went on :

" A tenderfoot hasn't much show if he once lets himself be drawn into a tin-horn's den," he remarked, in warning tones. " That is, if he's got money on him." I felt as if my friend Mr. Crocker's penetrating eye had been able to pierce through my clothing as far as those $300 in green-backs, in a nice soft chamois-leather belt which I wore under my shirt next my skin. " If they can't get him to play a game of cards and rob him that way, they're quite liable to club him, or dope him, or it might

be to shoot a hole in him, though shooting is liable to make too much noise."

" And you really mean to say, those crosses on the prairie were put up over murdered men ? " I queried.

" Yes," he said, " and over a few of their murderers too. You see, there's bound to be quite a few men buried there who simply slipped up in trying it on with the wrong man. You see, a skunk who is out to rob is liable to find himself mistaken in his victim. There's tenderfeet that can shoot."

I said nothing, but I was again conscious of that critical eye of his.

" Can you shoot ? " he went on.

" Yes, a little—with a rifle, that is," I answered guardedly. Of course I had been a Volunteer at Cambridge, but I thought it hardly worth while explaining all that. " And I've got a good gun, a 12-bore, double-barrel, by W. W. Greener, in my luggage," I added.

" Very good thing to have too sometimes," he said, with the air of a wise judge. " But a shot-gun's not very handy at close quarters, unless it's a sawed-off. For fighting in a bar-room, let me tell you, or on top of a stage-coach, they like to cut the barrels off a foot in front of the hammers, so the gun handles more like a pistol. Now you ain't got a pistol, have you ? "

I shook my head.

" And what's more, I'll lay you ain't got a pistol-pocket to carry one in those English pants you're wearing. Strictly, we're not supposed to carry

concealed weapons, but we all do it." He winked at me as he slued his right hip half round, so that I could see on it the diagonal line of the opening of a hip-pocket in his trousers with a peculiar lump below it inside. " That's what we call going heeled," he said.

" Oh, well then, I'm not heeled," I had to admit.

" There's quite a few men act like you even out West there," he nodded. "But I reckon it's best to go heeled on the off-chance. You never can tell——" He broke off and looked suddenly out of the window. " Look at there," he cried, " there's two Injuns right now watching this train. They'd scalp you in a holy minute, if you was to give 'em the chance."

And not a furlong away on the bare prairie stood two men on foot, holding their horses by the bridles, motionless as statues, watching us pass.

" Are those real Red Indians ? " cried I, much excited.

" Why certainly," he said. " You can tell that by the way they wear their blankets, and by the general look of 'em, though they're too far off to see their faces good. Red Cloud's got about 10,000 Sioux, more or less, somewhere around between here and the Yellow-stone River. And there are Arapa-hoes, and Cheyennes, and Kiowas, besides. They're all Plains Indians, and they're all hostiles, except when they come in every oncet in a while to their reservations and draw rations. But don't you let them catch you out here on the buffalo range, or they'll have your scalp quicker'n you can say

knife. That is, if they feel able to. They mostly leave a good strong train of waggons alone, but let 'em just drop on to some poor emigrant with a family in his waggon, or some unlucky hunter, who happens to have just shot off all his ammunition, and he's their meat."

" Then you mean to say," said I, " that those two men we saw standing so quietly there "—of course our train had left them miles behind by now —" would have scalped us if they could ? "

" Those Injuns ? You bet they would," returned Crocker. That's just all they live for, is scalps. Of course two Injuns like that, just by themselves, wouldn't be likely to do no great mischief. Two of them wouldn't dream of bothering this train. But it isn't so very long since a big war party of Sioux did actually derail a train—I think it was at Big Thompson—and they scalped a lot of chaps. One feller was a mule-skinner (that's a teamster, you understand) who was camped there, and he, as it happened, he wasn't plumb dead when they took his scalp, and he came to afterwards ; and just by luck, in the course of the fight, some other white man shot the Injun who had got his scalp, and recovered it, still fresh and bleeding. So when the whites had driven off the Injuns, they tried to put the scalp back on that mule-skinner's head, but 'twas no sort of use ; it wouldn't stick ! The man got well though, but now of course he has to wear a wig ! "

I really had to put up my hand to my head to feel if my own hair was still quite safe. It gave one

quite a new thrill to be told a horror like that almost
on the spot.

"I'll show you Big Thompson when we come
to it," said Crocker; "but it's like Julesburg
now—nothing but a section house left. There's no
town anywheres here along the railroad till we
get to Cheyenne. We're due there about 5 p.m.
and I'm getting off. You'll be getting off too, I
guess; that is, if you're bound for Denver as I
understood you to say."

Mr. Crocker was so friendly that I had taken
him freely into my confidence. My plans were
to get to Denver and get up as soon as possible
into the snow-slashed Sierras. As I told him, I
was going there for my health. I had been silly
ass enough to go for a ride on a hired horse I knew
nothing of, just before my final Cambridge exam;
the hireling had bolted and thrown me heavily
on my head. Result: a bad concussion, and six
months of constant headache; and when I got to
America the clammy heat in New York had made my
head feel much worse. But, by good luck, I came
across a book, by Bayard Taylor, just published,
Colorado, the Switzerland of America, and I felt by
instinct that the only chance for me was to go out
of these stifling Eastern cities up into the cool
keen air of the Rocky Mountains. And the Union
Pacific R.R., being now open, enabled me to gratify
my instinct—a thoroughly sound one—without
delay. In fact, only five days earlier I had been
sweltering at somewhere between 90° and 100°
in the shade, in the moist heavy air of Manhattan.

Now, 2000 miles west of there, out on the Plains, at an elevation of 5000 feet above sea level and breathing the dry air of the Great American Desert (in my old atlas the Great Plains were marked as The Great American Desert), already I felt very much better.

So when the conductor announced at last " Cheyenne, alight here for Stageline to Denver ! " I cheerfully alighted with Mr. Crocker from the cars, and went with him to what he said was the best hotel in town, and there the two of us had supper together. In those days Western meal hours were : breakfast, anywhere between 6 and 9 a.m. ; dinner, noon to 1 p.m., and supper, 5 to 7 p.m. After supper Crocker excused himself, saying that he had to go round town on business, so I sallied forth to explore my first Western town for myself.

Candidly, I cannot say that my first impression was good. The city seemed a desolate spot. Just a huddle of raw board houses, with a few more solid ones of brick here and there, dumped down on that everlasting yellow-brown prairie that we had traversed ever so many hundred miles of, since we left Omaha. Immediately outside, on the outskirts, were no gardens, or fields, or fences, or any sign of agriculture—just the bare, naked prairie, dotted here and there with a few camps of teamsters beside their white-tilted waggons, bull-whackers and mule-skinners, as Mr. Crocker had already taught me to call them. He said they brought their waggons in here to Cheyenne to load up with supplies that came out from the States over the newly opened

railroad for the mining towns in various parts of
Wyoming and Colorado Territories. Cheyenne was
the capital of Wyoming. Colorado lay directly
south of it and had no railroads as yet. I had a
good look at the teamsters. To me they seemed a
pretty rough lot, with their long boots, long hair,
and slouch hats, and I noticed that every single
one of them seemed to wear a heavy holster-pistol
belted on him. Perhaps they had smaller ones
besides in their hip-pockets, like my friend Crocker !
But, all alone by myself, I was too shy to ask them.

And then, coming in from the prairie, I saw a man
riding on a mustang ! I knew it must be a mustang
from my memories of Captain Mayne Reid's stories,
The Scalp Hunters and the rest. This mustang
was a small, active, wiry horse, with a long flowing
mane and tail, and a tripping sort of gait. The
man on him was dressed very much as the mule-
skinners were : he wore a broad slouch hat and
long boots outside his pants. I caught a keen
glance from him as he passed me, but there was so
much real kindness as well as keenness in his eye
that I plucked up heart to say :

" Oh, do you mind my asking—isn't that a
mustang ? "

His face expanded in a cheerful grin.

" Why yes," he said, " I guess so. But we do
call 'em broncos out here mostly. And this yer's
a California saddle," and he slapped his hand on
the horn. He saw how my eyes were fixed on the
knobbed horn that projected high above the front
of the saddle.

"What do you have that horn for?" I went on, as this new friend seemed so willing to be interviewed.

"That's for the lasso," was his reply. "If you rope a cow-brute on horseback, you can't hold nothing with your bare hands; what you got to do, is to take a turn of the rope around the horn of the saddle here, and then the horse does all the holding." He looked me over critically. "You just come off the cars, I reckon, ain't that so? Then I guess you never see no roping before? It's quite a trick, roping is, but you can't handle cattle and horses on these prairies without it."

My new friend was young though not very young, heavily bearded and uncommonly handsome; and my eye, ranging over him, saw not only his broad-brimmed hat and the pants tucked into the long boots, but also noticed very particularly the style in which he carried his big pistol. He wore his belt slack, so that it hung rather low on his right side; the butt of the pistol just showed at the top of the holster, and I noticed, too, that the lower end of the holster was provided with two long pieces of buckskin string, by which it was securely bound round his thigh.

"Why do you tie it like that?" I asked, making so bold as to touch the holster end.

"To keep it from joggling about too much when I'm riding at a lope," he replied. "A gun travels better so; and if ever you want to pull it, it pulls better so. Let me tell you that a ·44-calibre Colt is a heavyish thing to tote around." He seemed so

friendly that I thought I would get his opinion about pistol-carrying, to supplement Mr. Crocker's.

" Do you mind my asking you something else ? " I said. " Do you think I ought to carry a pistol now that I've come out here ? "

There was the quaint quizzical look on his face that I was already getting to know.

" Well," he said, speaking as gravely as a judge, " it's like this. You might tote a gun all around this Western country for twenty years and never want it. But, my friend, I can tell you this, if ever you did want it here, you'd want it powerful bad."

That phrase was a chestnut, as he must have known well enough, though I was too green to spot the fact ; but I came to know later on that " You'd want it powerful bad " had grown into a byword out West. However, the success of his chestnut seemed to him a good wind-up to our conversation. He raised his single curb-rein—tied as I noticed in a knot over his horse's withers—remarked " So long ! " and loped away. To " lope " was not hard to guess. It is a shortened form of the Spanish word " galopear " which the Western man had naturalized as American. I felt I had learned quite a lot as I walked back, well pleased with myself, to the hotel. Mr. Crocker was still out on business in the town, and I found that business hours might extend up to almost any time of night. However, he came in fairly early, and at once took me up into his room, and proposed to continue my education in the matter of pistols and how to handle them.

From the hip-pocket he had shown me, he produced a short bulldog-looking weapon, nickel-plated ; it worked with a double pull on the trigger, as he explained, demonstrating the merits of this special action by clicking it round with his thumb on the hammer and forefinger on the trigger. Suddenly —I couldn't say how—the horrid thing went off, and it went off while it was actually pointing my way, and I fairly jumped as the bullet passed within a few inches of my heart, just between my left arm and my side. The leaden missile lodged in the wall behind me, while Mr. Crocker's face went as white as a sheet.

" Oh, what an unlucky accident ! " he cried, so loud that it seemed as if he wanted to be heard in the next room. He looked at me very hard. " You're not hurt ? Really not ? Lord, but that was a close call ! I do feel ashamed of myself."

His apologies were loud and profuse. He passed his hands over my breast to make sure I was not wounded, while thought after thought raced through my whirling brain. Even as he passed those examining hands of his over my breast, I reflected that underneath were three hundred dollars, in my belt. I knew nothing of this Mr. Crocker, a mere chance acquaintance picked up on the cars. Suppose he were a thief, and after the dollars ! How easily he could have taken them if I had been killed.

And then I thought of my friend of an hour ago, on the mustang pony, and his meaning look at me when he said those words : " You'd want it

powerful bad!" Did I want it now? Could this be the sort of critical moment he had in mind? No, impossible! Crocker had thrown the deadly thing on the bed, and was only eager now to make quite absolutely sure I was not hurt. It was not in me to doubt his real sincerity. Nevertheless, here was I, a tenderfoot, all alone out in this new country, this Wild West, with its well-known and most deadly reputation for crimes of violence; and of course the odious suspicions would not quite go.

However, I declared myself satisfied with my friend's apologies; yes, and more than satisfied with this my first lesson on pistols and how to handle them. Quite enough to serve as an introduction to the peculiar ways of the Far West. And, still pursued by the worthy Crocker's excuses, I sought my virtuous couch, where I speedily forgot my suspicions, and managed to sleep perfectly sound my first night as a tenderfoot.

CHAPTER II

NEXT morning when I came down to breakfast in the Cheyenne hotel my friend Mr. Crocker was not visible.

" He's gone out early on business," so the clerk in the office informed me, which was only to be expected.

A live Western business man doesn't allow much grass to grow under his feet, and if he was going on by stage to Denver that afternoon he'd have to hustle. Well, if I must see Cheyenne without a chaperon, I had got one lesson from him yesterday, a lesson of sorts !

Uncertain what to try, I turned my steps towards a huge tent, rather like a circus tent, which with other smaller ones round it had located itself on the outskirts of Cheyenne city.

The attraction that drew me thither was the legend, " Professor MacDowell's Museum," visible from afar, for it was inscribed on the big tent roof in black letters a yard long. I wondered a little what sort of things they would have to show in the Cheyenne museum ; maybe geological specimens with ores from the mines, and perhaps dried plants and stuffed animals from the Rockies. Hopefully

I entered ; there seemed to be nobody about. Perhaps 9 a.m. was too early for the museum to be open. Presently, however, I plumped on to a rather washed-out, shifty-eyed, pallid youth, who stared hard at me with that same quizzical look I was quickly learning to recognize ; and it was disgustingly obvious how clearly he saw at first glance that here came a tenderfoot.

I remarked that I had just dropped in to have a look round.

" Right you are," he said ; and promptly he produced, for my benefit, not geological specimens but a pack of playing cards, and, shuffling them carelessly on a table that stood handy, he cut them a few times, turning up the bottom card of every cut for me to see.

" What'd you like ? " he queried. " Euchre ? All Fours ?   Poker ? "

" Oh, thank you," I said, drawing back a little. " No, I didn't want to play cards, but I thought your museum might have some curiosities that I'd like to see."

" That your game, eh ? " he said.   " Well, look in there, if you like.   I'll turn the handle."

Before me stood a sort of cabinet with a pair of glass lenses in it obviously intended for the eyes of anyone who wished to take a peep into a large stereoscope standing there. I peered in, but in the place of the scientific diagrams or views of specimens proper to a museum the youth proceeded to turn the handle and present me with something very much less proper, that is to say, picture after

picture of a lighted stage with a lot of half-dressed women on it.

" Very odd for a museum," thought I, and aloud I said, " Haven't you something more scientific ? Something more in touch with real life ? "

" Oh, if that's what you want ! " he exclaimed, evidently feeling that the words " real life " had given him my measure. And simply by shifting a lever he turned off the comparatively harmless actresses and turned on the first obscene pictures that my eyes ever beheld. They were absolutely impossible to describe, nauseous beyond words. Like a flash it burst on me that I was in a " dive," a den of thieves. People who kept things like that to show would stick at nothing, at no form of crime or villainy. This was one of the very places my kind friend Crocker had warned me of yesterday, the sort of place where you got murdered for your money. I thought of that forest of crosses at Julesburg standing over murdered men and I started back.

" Rather crude," I said, speaking quickly and trying to cover my alarm, while I looked anxiously behind me at the door to see if some ruffian had not already posted himself there, ready to " slug " me. But I could see no one, and in the twinkling of an eye I was at that big tent door, yes, and through it, and outside again.

" Here, where you off to so quick ? " called out the youth, running after me. " We can accommodate you whatever it is. If you don't see what you want, ask for it."

I knew very well what he wanted, those $300 I carried in greenbacks whose existence he doubtless suspected ; and up flashed again the overnight phrase of my other good friend, the mustang-pony man : " You'd want your pistol powerful bad." Here and now was what he had meant, and I realized how I was without a pistol, watching with intense sharpness to see if that young scoundrel was going to pull his weapon upon me. That he had one and was capable of using it I could not possibly doubt ; but, anyhow, I was no longer inside that den, Heaven be thanked ! I had escaped into the open air and the light of day. I had come out on to a public street of the capital city of Wyoming Territory. Surely now, at least, robbery under arms would be too outrageous. This last conjecture appeared to be right. The pallid youth flung a few jeering remarks in my direction, but he did not shoot, and he did not try to follow me farther.

" Museum, indeed," thought I.   " And six weeks ago I was in the Fitz-William at Cambridge ! "

Once fairly clear, I fled back to the very centre of the town, drawing in as I went long breaths of that most delicious air fresh from the Rockies. Faugh ! that den !

After such an experience something to soothe the nerves seemed indicated, namely a smoke. And here on the main street was a very neat and stylish tobacconist's store. The name over the door was Steinberger, of German origin doubtless. I went in and asked for a cigar. A spruce and

most obliging young man of Teutonic aspect but of unadulterated American speech supplied my wants. I lit up, and we got into conversation. I explained how I had come from across the water for my health and had only arrived last night at Cheyenne. Still considerably worked up by my recent experience at the surprising Museum of Professor MacDowell, I confided the story of it to young Steinberger, who was most sympathetic.

" Glad you got safe out of that," he said warmly. " There's a terrible low gang running that show. I don't think they'd have absolutely murdered you : that isn't exactly their game, or at least only as a last resort. But they'd have skinned you at cards in a holy minute, or doped your liquor, or any low-down game like that, to say nothing of the women they've got there."

He went on to give me much good advice and many cautions as to the dangers of these Wild Western cities, and I responded so warmly that presently I found myself accepting an invitation from him to come behind the counter and take a seat there where he kept a sort of snuggery and be introduced to his brother, Billy Steinberger.

And after a little while, business being very quiet and not a single customer appearing—" Very quiet place Cheyenne in the morning," said Billy the brother—the two tobacconists produced a pack of cards and proceeded to initiate me into the mysteries of " All Fours, Euchre, and Poker."

" Not for money," laughed Alf Steinberger, the one I had seen first, " not like your young friend

over there at the Museum. But if you're going to live out West you might as well know how the game's played."

So there we sat, and I was fast learning the science from my new friends, when there appeared through the doorway a good-looking, clean-shaven man in a coat so black and a shirt so white that he really seemed almost like a clergyman.

" 'Mornin', Alf," said he to my hosts, " Mornin', Billy. What's the matter with a good cigar ? "

" Mornin', Jake," said Alf and Billy together, Alf jumping up to serve him. I spotted this Mr. Jake's keen eyes bent on me and also on the card table. He did certainly look as smart as a whip. Alf remained standing behind the counter, rather obviously waiting for Jake to go, but the latter seemed in no hurry, though their conversation flagged. Finally I felt sure I saw Jake nudge Alf and heard him half whisper, " Introduce me to your young friend." Not very willingly Alf did so.

" Mr. Chisholm, let me introduce you to Mr. Townshend of Cambridge College, England, who has just come out here for his health."

At the name of England Jake Chisholm glanced at me with doubled interest.

" Mr. Townshend, sir, happy to meet you, sir." He extended a clean as well as a strong hand and grasped mine cordially. " You're English ; pleased to hear it ! My wife's English, and I'd like to have you meet her. If agreeable I'll take you round home to dinner at noon, and then you can

have a chat with her." I expressed much pleasure
in accepting. " I'll look in again presently," he
continued, " and call for you. I've just got a
little matter of business around the corner to attend
to first. So long, boys." And with a quick silent
step he was gone.

We three sat down again to our interrupted game.

" You don't know him of course," said Billy
to me, " but he's a gambler. One of the toniest
there is in Cheyenne too, I believe. They say
he plays a square game at his lay-out. Guess
he's just gone round there to see if everything's
all shipshape this morning. I don't guess he opens,
really, not till after supper, unless it was for a
very particular friend like you might be this afternoon."

There was that same everlasting quizzical grin
on Billy Steinberger's mug, the grin I was beginning
to get so tired of. Must I always go on being
such an obvious tenderfoot ?

" Well," cut in Alf, " if he wants you to start in
on poker or faro or any of these games, you're
not quite so green as you were. We've taught
you a thing or two, haven't we ? You're growing
quite fly ? " But the sarcasm, scarcely veiled,
showed both in voice and eyes.

" Thanks to you," answered I, " I do know
more than I did, but I don't feel exactly competent
to tackle a way-up Cheyenne gambler yet, even
supposing I wanted to." I was proud of working
in that " way-up."

" Oh, well," said Billy tolerantly, " likely enough

he'd treat you white. I've no quarrel with Jake Chisholm. No, sir, I guess he's as white a gambler as any you'd find around here. But as a general principle, with gamblers as well as some other sorts, you just keep your eye skinned, and don't you forget it."

And right there the first thing that occurred to me was that I might begin by keeping a wary eye on this pair of German-American gentlemen, for it struck me that they were a little afraid of being given away by a tenderfoot, as I was, to such a right good customer of theirs as Mr. Jake Chisholm.

In short my tobacco-selling friends wanted to hedge.

A little before twelve o'clock Jake returned, his business done, and carried me off.

There was a real warmth of friendliness about the man that fairly won my heart, and I told him of my being taken in by the high-sounding title of Professor McDowell's Museum, as I had told the Steinbergers. He did laugh !

" Why, it's one of the lowest dives around town," he said, " and I am damned glad you got safe out of it. They're a real low down lot there, folks that 'ud skin a flea for his hide and tallow."

" I suppose they go on more or less all night there," I said, " and the reason I ran on to nobody but that boy was that the others were sleeping it off ? "

" That's jes' about the size of it." He nodded approvingly. " Say, you was quite right not to

play with our friends back there in the store for money. I suppose you didn't ? That is, anyway, I didn't see any money put up. Of course you understand that I don't mean to say they're thugs like that McDowell outfit ; but they're on it all right."

"What's ' on it,' " I wanted to know. Jake was so friendly that I didn't mind asking him to translate.

" ' On it ' ? Oh, on the make, out to win, and always looking for a dead sure thing, that's being ' on it.' Why, them chaps had got it fixed all right for you if you'd ever put up the spondulics " —clearly the cash—" Why, you was as innocent of spotting it as a two-year-old baby, but they'd got a looking-glass there in the cover of an open cigar box, right behind you inside that show-case, so as they could see every card in your hand ! You didn't spot that ? "

" No, indeed," I replied. " I never thought of such a thing."

" Oh, well," he said tolerantly, " there's a heap worse things bin' done than that at cards ; but that mirror dodge is one of the safest and simplest, if you can only work it. But, for you, the best dodge of all will be jes' to leave 'em alone—the cards, I mean. I'm a professional gambler, as I guess them fellers will have told you ; but I feel kind of friendly to you coming out fresh here from my wife's country, and that's my advice to you. ' You leave 'em alone.' "

" Thank you very much," I said ; " I'm sure

you're right, and you may trust me not to forget it."

" You was at Cambridge College ? " went on my new friend. " Leastways that's how I understood Alf to say. Was you so ? "

" Oh, yes," I replied, repeating once more my explanation of how I came to Wyoming.

" Wal', sir," rejoined Jake, " I guess as how they must have learned you a 'hull lot there at college. But "—reflectively—" you English folks has a thing or two to learn yet, when you get out here. Take my wife for instance. Her folks, back there in England was took in by them Mormon missionaries as Brigham Young sends out. Them fellers made the pore innocents over yonder believe as the Mormons were the true Saints and Brigham Young the Prophet of God, and that Salt Lake City wasn't nothing else than heaven on earth. And so they come over, with a 'hull crowd of Mormon converts like 'emselves, yes, a 'hull shipload of 'em, to Salt Lake. And they found, or some of 'em found anyways, that instead of heaven it was jes' hell. That's what my wife did. She was an innocent young gal. And they went and married her (what they called marrying) to a golderned old Mormon Elder that had a dozen wives already. She hadn't learned nothing of that kind in England, and she didn't like it. But she dursn't kick. Nothin' was too bad for Mormons to do if anyone ever dared to quit them. They was hard enough on Gentiles, anyhow, but when it came to a Mormon quittin' the fold, Scott !

but they was just p'ison. There was gangs of 'em, Danites, and Avenging Angels, and I dunno how many more, that stuck at nothing in the way of tortures. Red Injuns is pretty good at tortures, but they ain't in it with the Avenging Angels."

" Then how on earth did she escape ? " I asked.

" Oh, well," he said, " we fixed that up, her and me did." His lips wore a wily smile as he looked at my innocent face.

" But how did you ever come across her there ? " I asked him. " You weren't a Mormon, were you ? "

" Not much, me ! " The lips broadened into a grim laugh. " No, sir, I come to Salt Lake, me, with Colonel Connor's Command of Volunteers from California. I wasn't one of the California Volunteers myself, but I kept a lay-out for 'em at Camp Douglas. That's the fortified camp we had, right there over Salt Lake City. We could have thrown hot shot into Brigham's backyard, if we'd wanted, and we was mighty nigh doing it once or twicet. Wal', as I was sayin', I kept a lay-out there, and most of us of the Command used to drop into the Salt Lake stores when we wanted to trade, and tried to be as friendly with the Mormons as we knew how. There was a good few Gentile stores in Salt Lake too, but even there most all the folks who went to trade was Mormons. An' that was how I run acrost her buying suthin' in a store. We got talking together and kind of took to one another first start. Then we got to meetin'—quite casually you understand," with

another very knowing smile. " We fixed it to meet at one store one day and another the next time, like that. And I got regularly stuck on her, and she let out to me as how she jes' loathed the 'hull Mormon show, and was fair sick to get away. 'Course I told her I'd fix things for her, and "—again that knowing glance—" you bet I did."

" Oh," said I in all simplicity, " did you arrange a divorce ? " To the Englishman of the sixties the facility for divorces in America was a decidedly familiar, not to say comic, idea.

" Divorce, hell ! " he returned grimly. " Not by a jugful. Who wants any divorce ? Them Mormon marriages don't amount to nuthin'. Plural marriages ain't lawful in these yere United States. No, it wasn't that I had to fix for. But them Mormons jes' went raging mad over any interference with their women. Why, I can tell you they jes' used to . . ."

I cannot print here the unspeakable atrocities which he told me were practised on any man caught invading the " rights " of a Mormon " husband." He fairly made me shudder before he got through, and he saw it.

" I don't wonder that shocks you," said he. " All the same I had to take my chances. And she was as brave as they make 'em, but I had to plan to save her. I wasn't going to have her made a victim of their Blood Atonement, a vile scheme they had for punishing the women. This was how we done the trick. I used to meet her,

as I said, casual-like at various stores, and a few
words, either spoken or just written on a scrap
of paper maybe, did the arranging. Wal', I had
lots of good friends among them old Californians
of the Command, and they got me a suit of soldier
clothes that I guessed would fit her. And I went
of a dark night and dropped 'em into the yard of
that golderned old Elder's house, so she'd be
able to get 'em : 'course we fixed it all to rights
first very careful. I dunno how she worked it
to hide the things in the house, where of course
there was the other wives watching her. But
she managed it. And then the next night she
slipped out, and got into the soldier clothes, and
got over the fence and into my arms that was
watching for her. I had a U.S. cavalry horse
with a McClellan saddle borrowed a-purpose. I'd
got two of my best friends to take my own horses
and saddles on to the Wyoming Boundary, a good
eighty miles, I reckon ; and more friends to be
waiting for us half-way with good cavalry horses
we made bold to borrow off Uncle Sam. Wal',
it all went like clockwork. I took her up in the
saddle, me sitting on the crupper behind ; luck
was with us and we got safe up to outside Camp
Douglas without being ever seen or interfered
with. There I had another friend with a horse
ready, so we had a horse apiece. We rode like
Old Harry for Echo Cañon, and our luck held
good. There was a fine moon after ten o'clock
—'course I had allowed for that. But there was
no being held-up by any guards or anything, as

there might have been easily enough. A hold-up was what no man couldn't allow for, 'cept by being well heeled, and having a good soldier friend go along the first half of the road ! No, we never was held up oncet ! You bet I was thankful. And we got safe to the friends with fresh horses, and so on to them that had my own horses jes' over the Boundary in Wyoming. They went back with the cavalry horses, and you bet they carried my blessing. We felt safer once we was across in Wyoming, and we took it easier on into Bridger. But it was the devil's own ride for a young woman. Only she was clar' grit, you bet, grit clar' down to her boots."

" And did you stop on there in Bridger ? " said I, keen to hear the end of this exciting Far Western elopement.

" Not much, Mary Anne ! " came his laughing correction. " We did rest thar' two days, for she was plumb tired out, and I knowed it'd take them Avengers that much time, or maybe more, to find out which way we'd gone and to get on our trail. But I wanted to put 1000 miles and not 100 between me and them Avenging Angels. So soon as she was a little rested we hit the trail again, and this time we kept a-moving till we got up to Virginia City, Montana. We felt pretty safe there, and there we got married. Virginia City was a place that suited me and my game right enough. You see I'm a professional gambler "—he said this as before without the slightest embarrassment—" and Alder Gulch was fairly booming. I reckon there

was five thousand miners there taking out $10 a day to the man, most of 'em. Naturally I done well enough till the Gulch played out, and then I come on down here to Cheyenne. And right here's where we live." He halted before a neat frame house on a side street and ushered me inside.

Mrs. Chisholm looked still quite young, and she had managed to keep the English roses in her cheeks so bright, in spite of all she had been through, that I could not wonder at Jake's having fallen in love at first sight. But I failed to get much conversation out of her about England. Her people were from the North, which I hardly knew, and, as far as I could judge, had been in humble circumstances there.

" Tell us about Cambridge College," cut in Jake as I was feeling round for a fresh opening; " how long was you there ? "

" Four years," I answered, and willingly taking his cue I went on to tell of the 'Varsity Sports, and the Boat-race, as well as of a few of our lighter amusements in college. Jake was amused by the small undergraduate larks I recounted, such as the crutch races round the New Court of Trinity, when I was on crutches for a month from a gymnasium accident and the men used to borrow my crutches and those of another undergrad who was lame and extemporized races in college under cover of night. Remembering Jake's profession I told also of 1868 and the story of Hermit's Derby, when that great horse (who was supposed to be on the sick list) won at 50 to 1 against. E——,

a Trinity man whom I knew, had a private tip and put a tenner on Hermit at those odds last thing. Of course he stood to win £500, but unfortunately the firm of bookmakers with whom he had placed the bet proved to be defaulters and he never got paid. Jake smiled grimly.

" He'd orter hev' gone for 'em with a gun," he said.

" Oh, that's not done in England," I returned. " And as betting's not legal it wasn't recoverable by law. And, besides, if he had gone to law, the dons would have heard about it and sent him down."

" 'Scuse me sayin' it," said Jake, " but are the most of them undergraduates as innocent as you do look to be ? For it's God's truth I'm telling you, you do look a perfect innocent. But don't you reckon as that friend of yourn was a blamed fool to bet at all under them conditions ? "

" Well, I suppose he was," I had to admit. " And, besides, he probably might have come out all right if he'd just stuck to Spot Sanderson, who was our local bookmaker, as you may say. I didn't bet myself, but Spot Sanderson used to be down by the course when the May races were on (those were the college boat-races you know) and you could back your college boat if you'd a fancy to. Or you could bet with him on the Sports, or the Oxford race, or anything. And he always paid, so they said at least."

Jake was fairly tickled at the idea of a professional gambler attaching himself to what he would persist in calling Cambridge College.

" Say, Annie," he cut in to his wife, " what's the matter with our going there for a trip ? Mebbe I'd graduate some of them old dons as Mr. Townshend talks of—get 'em to set up a new College Chair of Poker, just for a little variety on their mouldy Hebrew-Greek, what say ? "

But Annie didn't rise to the suggestion, though she could not help smiling a little. Jake as the Professor of a new Chair at Cambridge was irresistible.

Then I went on to tell of my journey out to America, and of New York and Boston, Chicago and Cheyenne. But when I told how Mr. Crocker had so very nearly killed me overnight while trying to exhibit the correct manipulation of that hippocket pistol Jake's hearty whole-souled laugh rang right out.

" Calls hisself a Western man, does he ? " he scoffed. " Why, you hear me talk, I'll lay as he ain't nuthin' but a Chicago drummer. A Chicago drummer ! " he repeated with the withering scorn of the Man from California. " Trust him for messing about with a man's weapon. 'Scuse my saying so, if he's a friend of yourn, but Lord ! what a damn fool trick that was of his ! I'm reel glad he didn't plug you, but it's a plumb wonder you're alive." He looked at my empty plate and coffee-cup—Mrs. Chisholm gave us coffee with our meal, no alcoholic drinks. " Through ? Then come on out into the backyard and I'll show you a thing or two before you're a day older. Can't learn too soon."

So to the backyard we adjourned, and Jake produced several pistols ranging from a Colt ·44 calibre to a derringer, and he showed me how to handle each of them individually. Good and very practical was his teaching; so much so that it struck me that never at Cambridge had I come across a don whose method was better. The way he made you use your head first, and then combine theory with practice was simply perfect. He had a real genius, and I have known occupants of certain University Chairs who might have taken a hint from him with profit.

To aim low, but not too low, to keep your eye on the mark more than on the sights, to pull the very instant you get on, and to pull with one very firm, very quick, squeeze of the finger, to get your aim while your weapon is coming up, and not waste time by first bringing it up perpendicular, and then lowering it. But there; the theory is all in the textbooks nowadays, so why repeat it here? The real difficulty is to put theory into practice; and there each man has to be his own teacher in the last resort. In short, as the wise Jake put it, " It's up to yourself."

However, I profited much by this Far Western Professor's advice that afternoon, and I fired a number of shots with his various weapons, and he was good enough to call me a promising pupil. Finally I took my leave of Mrs. Chisholm and departed to the hotel to see about getting my luggage aboard the stage for Denver; but I did not get rid of my friendly gambler. He fairly

shepherded me around Cheyenne all that afternoon, watchful to see that I didn't put my foot into it anywhere, or with anybody, and still giving me occasional bits of advice that were most unquestionably sound. He never left me, in fact, not till it was the correct time for Wells Fargo's four-horse stage to start.

The last thing I remember of him is the wistful smile on that friendly face of his as he warmly pressed my hand after I had climbed aboard. He put his mouth close to my ear and he whispered longingly :

" Lord, man, if I only had your mug ! "

CHAPTER III

THREE PER CENT

I WISH I could remember more of that first Western stage drive from Cheyenne to Denver. There were several of us passengers on Wells Fargo's coach, but the man who caught my attention from the first was the coachman or stage-driver, who was Bill Updike. He was a singular being : his closest attention was fixed unremittingly upon the horses he controlled so deftly with the four lines, the word he used for reins, held in his two hands, the near reins in his left, the off in his right ; but he kept the other side of his brain free as air for lively and humorous talk with his passengers. I was by no means the only tenderfoot on board, and for all of us alike Bill did the honours of the new Territory we had just entered, as he himself would have put it, in ·A number 1 style. From Cheyenne the road ran due south for over a hundred miles, keeping parallel the whole way to the main range of the Rocky Mountains; Long's Peak, thirty miles to the west was by far the highest of them that we could see, rising as it did to an elevation of nearly 15,000 feet, or some 9000 above the road we were travelling. Between this great peak and the Plains rose endless minor mountain

ranges mostly from 8000 to 12,000 feet high, while
the road itself took its course out on the Plains,
still farther to the east so as to avoid the almost
impassable mountain gorges. Rocky mountains they
truly were, both in name and nature. Their sides,
when not bare rock, showed dark with pines ; but,
east of them, where our road ran, the country consisted of bare treeless rolling downs covered with
yellow grass, which Bill informed us was cured
by the sun as regular as the year went round into
natural hay of the finest quality.

" It's a godsend to the bull-whackers," he said.

" What are bull-whackers ? " I inquired.

" Why, yonder's some of 'em now," he exclaimed,
and as he spoke he pulled his team to the right so
that the stage swung violently to one side out of
the track, and lo ! there on our left walked a great
string of six pairs of yoked oxen, having their
yokes attached by a long heavy iron chain to the
tongue or pole of the front one of two white-tilted
waggons coupled one behind the other. Alongside
the aftermost of the six pairs of oxen, the pair that
had the waggon-tongue made fast to their yoke,
there moved slowly a slouch-hatted man on foot,
carrying a whip with a tapering lash, the middle of
which looked to me to be thicker than his wrist
and the length of it near twenty feet. We galloped
past his team and a dozen more six-yoke teams just
like it. Along the road in front went one man
riding a saddle pony. He was the waggon boss,
I was informed. The road was nothing more than
a broad strip of bare earth with the grass worn off

it, and marked with parallel lines of tracks left by wheels.   On either side spread the grass-grown prairie far as eye could see.

" Them's bull-whackers," said Bill.   " Of course you can see the teams are oxen not bulls, but that's what they call 'em all the same, and you can bet your sweet life every pound of freight that comes to this territory comes on them waggons or on those of the mule-skinners."

" I guess they'll be the drivers of mule teams," I interjected.   Already I was learning to say " I guess."

" Right, first time ! " he grinned back : he liked having a pupil.

" But how does the bull-whacker steer ? " I asked.   " He hasn't any reins that I can see."

" Oh, he does it all with his voice," said Bill. " He talks to 'em like humans.   They know.   He tells 'em, ' Gee, gee there, you sons of biscuits,' and the leaders swing right, quick's they can, and the rest of the bull-team follows suit.   If he says ' Woo-haw, Woo, come-haw,' they come haw— that's left—as quick as winking ; or if they don't they know it.   The bull-whacker jumps three steps forward and swings that fifteen foot whip and pops it across their sterns till them leaders learn what's what.   Oh, the bull-whacker knows his game."

The coach swung out again to pass another bull-train : the whole road to Denver was lined with them seemingly.

" One of the very first lot of bull-teams that ever crossed the Plains," so Bill told us, " was caught

ten years ago, in 1859 that was, near Golden, in a
fall blizzard. The bull-whackers knew perfectly
well that their bulls was bound to freeze to death
if they was held around the waggons without shelter,
so the waggon boss turned them loose to shift for
themselves ; he thought the odds was 100 to 1
he'd never set eyes on 'em again.

" The waggons was completely snowed up ; winter
set in ; and the men, who had plenty of grub, just
camped right there till it should come spring :
they couldn't get back, so there was nothing else
for 'em to do. Spring come at last, and the boss
saddled up his horse ; his horse was alive still, for
through all the storms they had kept him going
by blanketing him under the lee of a waggon and
giving him a little of the flour and cornmeal they
had along ; also they pulled dry grass for him to
eat, so he had come through all right. The boss
circled around striking off in a southerly direction ;
for he knowed as cattle allus is bound to drift south
in winter ; he thought mebbe he'd find their
skeletons, or as much anyway as the wolves had
left of 'em. Instead he found the 'hull lot of
bulls, alive and safe, in the timber, on Plum Creek,
on this side of the Divide ; and not only was they
alive ; but they was plumb fat. The timber had
giv' 'em shelter, and they'd lived fine on the natural
sun-cured hay. The waggon-boss rode back to
his camp with the news. ' Boys,' says he, ' it's a
miracle, nuthin' less, and this here is God's country
sure. They're fat ! ' "

I did not know enough then about how cattle

are raised to tumble to the full significance of this story (which was quite true), but there were men on the coach who saw what it meant, and I learned that they took it to imply that the whole of the Great Plains, say 2000 miles from north to south and 500 miles from east to west, would become one vast cattle range whenever the wild buffalo and the Red Indians were disposed of. This was an idea on so magnificent a scale that it excited me vastly, and I stored it away in my mind, to bring forth fruit later.

Our road, as I have said, ran parallel, on the Plains, to the great mountain chain ; consequently it crossed at right angles the valleys of the numerous creeks running out from the range eastwards to join the South Platte. Those names still haunt my memory, Cache-la-poudre, Big Thompson, Little Thompson, St. Vrain's Fork, Boulder, Coal Creek, Clear Creek—names in which romance and realism were quaintly intertwined.

In these valleys pioneer settlers had taken up farms and started to grow potatoes and wheat on the bottom lands by irrigation ; in every valley ditches for this purpose were taken out from the main Creek farther up than the land to be watered near where the Creek emerged from the mountains ; and the ditch line being led along the sloping valley-side with a gradient of not more than six or eight feet to the mile was soon far above the main creek below at the valley-bottom which had a fall of perhaps forty or fifty. But when the stage first came into sight of one of these valleys and you looked

right down from above into it, the effect to the eye was that the valley-bottom below you lay there as level as a floor, so the ditch line running out along the valley-side and now having manifestly gained an elevation of perhaps a hundred feet above the bottom in the course of two or three miles looked exactly as if it had been running uphill. It was the strangest optical illusion, exhibited not in a conjurer's show but in the open air, that ever I saw, and it struck the other men in the same way.

I regret to say Bill Updike was not above pulling our legs.

" Queer, ain't it ? " he said. " That's what makes irrigation so simple in this new Territory of Colorado. Water runs uphill just as well as down. Effect of the light air. We're a whole mile above sea level here, and the air pressure ain't half of what it is back there in New York ! "

I might be a tenderfoot, and my University degree had undoubtedly been obtained in classics not in science, but I couldn't quite swallow that. What amused me was our stage-driver Bill's absolutely serious voice, and likewise the serious way in which some of our wise men from the East whom we had aboard took it ; they had heard many strange things about the West, but that water should run uphill, not in a force-pipe but in an open irrigating ditch, that was a large order. They hesitated to believe, but at the same time they were extremely puzzled. I simply said :

" Water never ran uphill yet."

" Oh, thar' ain't no doubt about it," went on Bill

in the same confident serious voice. " Look right there, before your eyes, and you can see the 'hull thing for yourselves. It's only another of the miracles of God's Country."

If ever a new country had a good backer (and a good backer is what a new country wants) it was Colorado Territory when she rejoiced in the great Bill Updike.

But there was another man on the stage who was of much more importance to Colorado than Bill, and he smiled approval at my denial. I had found a backer, and one apparently who counted. He was a tall spare-built man with grizzled beard and moustache ; he was no longer young, but the fire in his flashing eyes showed him to be still full of life. I wondered who he was, as he fairly poured it out to Bill.

" That's one of the most remarkable men we've got," said the man sitting next me in a low voice so as not to be overheard. " That's Governor William Gilpin. He was the first Governor of Colorado, and you might call him its first founder. He's a real curiosity : he's of Quaker stock, and yet he went to West Point and he became a Cavalry colonel and fought in the Mexican war. He'd have been senior officer to Grant and Sherman if only he'd stayed on, but he resigned to become a pioneer and ex- plorer. He's brainy. It was his great idea that placed Colorado a-straddle of the backbone of the continent so that one-half of the rivers in this Territory run to the Pacific and half to the Atlantic. He's eloquent about making the Great Sierra unite the two halves

of the continent instead of dividing them. Oh,
you'll hear him talk ; he's a wonder when he lets
himself go, and he's not unwilling to do it too.
And he writes even loftier than he speaks. Maybe
you'd call it highfalutin, but there's the real stuff
in it. Just now he's by way of being poor. He's
a pure man : he must have had a thousand chances
to enrich himself when he was Governor of Colorado
in the days when the mines were booming, but he
didn't use 'em. What he did do was this : as a
pioneer he obtained a fine Spanish grant of a block
of land down in the San Luis Park ; it's called the
Sangre de Cristo grant. I guess there's a million
acres in it : it's huge. But just now it don't bring
in nothing ; it's undeveloped ; it's away back of
beyond. Some day when we get railways and tele-
graph lines and white folks to settle up that part
of the country, it'll be worth millions, but that
day ain't yet. He knows it too, and he won't sell
cheap ; he believes in the future, no man more,
and he prefers to wait. But in the meantime he's
skin-poor. I suppose you could hardly believe
that ? "

" Indeed I can," said I, " and I am truly proud
to have such a backer. You know him, it seems :
won't you introduce me ? " and I told him my
name and who I was.

By this time the Governor had polished off Bill
Updike, so my friendly neighbour performed the
introduction. Governor Gilpin received me cordially, shook hands, and at once began to hold forth
on what most particularly interested him just now,

namely the exploration of the Grand Cañon of the Colorado River.

" The greatest gash on the earth's surface, Mr. Townshend," said he impressively. " It is 500 miles in length and a mile in vertical depth. The walls are a series of precipices rising to that amazing height. Never has it been traversed by mortal man. Dead bodies of Indian braves have been washed down it, bodies of Utès or Navajos, or Apaches, slain in their intertribal wars and given to the current, but never yet has any living human being passed that way. Now, for the first time, the attempt is being made. That grand explorer, Major Powell, despite his having only one arm—he lost his right arm in the war—has dared it with his brave companions, and to-day they are trying to navigate that wild water in craft specially constructed for the purpose. May God give them success ! But I have my fears : more than two months have now elapsed since the party disappeared into the chasm, and no word of their fate has ever reached the outer world. The torrent may have swallowed them up ; the Indians may have destroyed them ; their boats may have been wrecked with the loss of all their provisions, and they may consequently have been starved to death ; we know nothing. You tell me your idea is to travel through this Territory ; let me beg of you to keep these explorers in your mind and to lose no opportunity of finding out, whether from miners or trappers or Indians, whatever there is to be known of their fate."

I assured him that I would take the greatest pains to learn what I could. He went on :

" The present governor of this Territory, Gen. Edward M. McCook, proposes to visit the Los Pinos Agency for the Southern Utes, which is just being established on a fork of the Gunnison River, across the range, which flows ultimately to the Colorado. If you happened to accompany him the opportunity to find out something might be granted you."

" Nothing I should like better," said I, " but I think my first move must be not quite so far. I want to go and see a friend that I have, a mining engineer who is up at Central City. But if I can I'd like well to make the trip you suggest later on."

" I'm glad to hear you speak so," said the Governor warmly. " You must come round and talk it over with me in Denver, Mr. Townshend. You'll find me at Mr. D. A. Cheever's office on Larimer Street : I use it as my own when I'm in town."

Yes, this owner of a million acres used a friend's office and didn't mind admitting it. He certainly was a character.

The stage got to Denver at last, and I put up at an hotel recommended to me, the American House.

I wrote at once to Ally Hodges, my mining engineer friend. Last year he had paid a visit to Cambridge on his way back to America from Germany where he had been studying, and I had made friends with him there. Since then we had exchanged letters,

and I wanted to get up to Central City if, as I had reason to believe, he was there.

Meantime I called on Governor Gilpin at the address he had given me, and was duly introduced to the Governor's friend, Mr. David Augustus Cheever, a real-estate owner who was holding on for a rise in Denver lots, and there also I met his two brothers, Charles Cheever, likewise interested in real estate, and Ned Cheever, who had a small ranch up the Platte. The three were New Englanders and were devoted friends of the Governor, whom they admired immensely. They were all three of them bachelors, middle-aged, and moderately prosperous. Nobody seemed to be very prosperous in Denver just then : indeed, the capital city of the Territory had only about 5000 inhabitants and seemed to be a bit down on its luck. The mines were not paying at all well, freights were very high, making everything so expensive, and the railroad had not come.

" But it's coming, and coming soon, Mr. Townshend," said Gus Cheever very hopefully, " and then you'll see things here hum."

" I hope they will hum," I said cordially. " Speaking for myself I may say I didn't exactly come out here to invest here, but it's depressing to be in a country that's down on its luck."

" Well, we're not going to be down on our luck in this office," said Gus. " How could we with such a man as Governor Gilpin around ? And I hope you'll make this office your home, Mr. Townshend, whenever you're in Denver. The-

door's on the latch and the string hangs outside."

This was a truly Western way of expressing
hospitality, and I felt that it was really meant.
Mr. D. A. Cheever and I became great friends and
I have the warmest recollection of his kindness.

Money arrangements I had also to see about,
and my next step was to present my credentials
at one of the Denver banks to which I had been
careful to bring an introduction from a firm of
good standing " back East." The first thing I did
was to get rid of most of the $300 I carried in my
belt by opening an account and putting the money
on deposit. My brief Cheyenne experience had
taught me how unpleasant it was to feel oneself
rather too well worth robbing. And the next thing
I did was to have an interesting interview with the
bank-manager, or as Americans call him the cashier.
He was a busy man, but he managed to find time
to have a chat with a new-comer from the Old
Country ; for the thing that Colorado particularly
wanted just then above all others was capital ; and
capital might just as well come from overseas as
from " back East." I told him I had some capital,
not a great deal, that I could bring over, and I
was anxious to know what sort of returns I might
expect for it.

" I should like to know the usual rate of interest
here," I said.

" Well, it varies of course," he answered. " Your
own knowledge of finance must tell you that."

My knowledge of finance indeed ! It consisted

so far in my having inherited a little money and lived on the interest of that and an allowance.

" Interest here," continued the banker, " varies according to the security. But you may take it, roughly speaking, at 3 per cent."

" Three per cent ! " I exclaimed, much surprised. " Why, I can do better than that in England.   I've got mine invested there at 4½ or 5.   Why, over there I could get 3 per cent simply by putting it in consols."

" Ah, but," smiled the banker, " you're thinking of 3 per cent per annum, while I'm talking of 3 per cent a month."

My knowledge of finance was indeed ignorance in Colorado.

And on inquiry elsewhere I found that the Denver banker was absolutely right : 3 per cent a month, and that only on good security, was the rate of interest in the Far West then current. And if the offered security was merely personal it might easily be as much as 5 per cent.   The thought was enough to make the mouth of a Jew water !   I myself, however, not being of Jewish blood, was in no hurry to seize the fine opportunity thus offered —I have often wished since I had.   What I wanted was in the first place to get quite well, and secondly to see more of this extraordinary new country before I did anything in the way of investing.

I got an answer from Ally Hodges next day, in which he proposed that I should run up to Central City as soon as possible and see him, for he did not think he should stay on in Colorado much longer.

I settled to do this at once, and another stage-coach
journey, happily not of twenty-two hours' dura-
tion, however, took me to Central City, where I
found Hodges. We were glad to see each other
again, but I found him rather despondent about
the mining future of Colorado. Indeed, I did not
wonder when I saw so many mining-shafts closed
and stamp-mills idle. Denver, as I had already
seen, was dull, waiting for the railway to come and
wake things up, but what were the miners waiting
for ?

Well, the answer was that the surface ores were
pretty much worked out by this time : they had
been partly oxidized (I was no engineer, but this
was how I understood it) and so could be treated
effectively in stamp-mills. Now the mines had got
deeper and the ores were refractory sulphurets,
which the common stamp-mill could make nothing
of, and what they were waiting for was a new process. It was up to somebody to invent some new
dodge, and lo ! in no time Central and Black Hawk
and the rest of the mining towns would boom again.
Alas, I was not the much needed inventor ! A
classical education doesn't fit one for dealing with
refractory sulphurets. Even Hodges, the trained
engineer, didn't feel equal to it.

" I'm off to Utah," he told me. " I don't see
any opening here. Utah may have one, and, if
not, then I guess I'll try Nevada. They have been
at it longer there, and they've got a railroad now.
And what I learned in Germany may be of more
use there than here."

" Look here," I said, " people talk about the good fishing and hunting there is here in the mountains. Don't you want to go off and have a trip here first ? "

" Can't afford the time," he said. " But this I can do. I'll introduce you to a friend of mine here, Mr. Bastow. He owns one of the stamp-mills that still have got non-refractory ores to run upon, and I know he wants a holiday."

So I was duly introduced to Mr. Bastow, whom I found a most pleasant and friendly man, and he asked me to go with him on a fishing trip over to the creeks on the head of Boulder River. I gladly accepted, hired for myself a horse, and accompanied him. Bastow had along as cook one of his hired men from the mill which was not running on full time, and he also had with him an old trapper named Ed, as hunter.

A very jolly week of it we had, camping in the mountains, feasting on Rocky Mountain trout and grouse ; I had brought out a settler's double gun by W. W. Greener of Birmingham : this was a muzzle-loading smoothbore, with 30-inch barrels and a weight of about 9 lb., and it was made to shoot round bullets twelve to the pound for big game as well as small shot and buckshot ; though a trifle heavy, it served its purpose well. Round the camp fire, old Ed told us great stories of Indians and of the " mountainee men " of the old days. It was barely ten years since the discovery of gold in Colorado, and before then the whole country from the Missouri River to California was absolute wilderness.

" I suppose a whole lot of that country over the mountains there is still unexplored ? " I said.

" Yes, it is," answered the trapper with a chuckle. " And what's more, it's likely to stay unexplored. There's the Grand Cañon now. That's just below the Ute country—they're Paiutes down in there. And Gov'ment's got an outfit out there right now explorin' ! A lot of men from the States, men from Chicago and back East "—there was infinite scorn in the trapper's voice—" say as they're going to explore the Grand Cañon ! Explore hell ! Hell's the country they'll explore. No man's ever bin down the Grand Cañon, and never will. Not alive. Mebbe a corpse might get through : that's what Douglas—he's a Ute chief—said to me. ' Them canoes go bust,' he says. ' Water buck heap ! Canoe—Ugh,' and he makes signs—Injuns talk a heap with signs—with his hands showing jes' how the boats they've made are bound to get knocked to bits. Major Powell, that's his name, he's the Gov'ment man as has built the boats upon Green River. I guess he's started by now to go down the Cañon. And by now I guess he's drowned, he and his men. Goners they are, I'll bet, the last one of 'em. That is unless they've crawfished, and turned their boats loose, and crawled out into Utah or Arizona by one of them side Cañons."

" Then nobody knows where they are now ? " I said.

" No," he returned, " and nobody ain't likely to know for a whiles yet. If they're drowned, they're drowned, and nobody'll never know the rights

of it. If they do manage to crawl out we shall hear from 'em right enough sometime, but not till away along in the fall, I guess."

Of course I remembered what Governor Gilpin had said of Major Powell's Grand Cañon expedition ; he had told me to look out for any information about it, but I did not see much chance here, and I could not help being struck by the extreme contempt displayed for the explorers by our Old Man of the Mountains. But when thirty-four years later I myself went down by Captain Hanse's trail to the bottom of the Grand Cañon with Professor T. Mitchell Prudden of Columbia, and when in that awful chasm I looked up at the mile-high walls of naked rock on either side I could not but feel the deepest respect for Powell and his little band of heroes who first had dared to traverse the unknown depths of that terrific gash in the earth's surface.

I enjoyed that fortnight's fishing trip with Mr. Bastow and old Ed immensely, and the outdoor life and the pure keen air of the Rockies did my aching head a world of good. However, the pleasantest things have to come to an end at last ; we returned to Central City where I said good-bye to Bastow and also to Ally Hodges, and I took the stage once more back to Denver, which I made my head-quarters. There, in the shop of Carlos Gove, a gunsmith, I did actually run across the Governor of Colorado, General McCook, but I was too shy to introduce myself to him. This was how it happened. I had struck up quite a friendship with Gove, an elderly man very keen on guns of all sorts. I went to him to

buy a pistol and had provided myself with a navy
Colt, a ·36-calibre muzzle-loading six-shooter, with
which I practised at the butt in Gove's backyard,
along with his boy Tom, with whom I made great
friends. Also I lent my Greener gun to Gove,
who wanted to copy some part of it for his own
purposes. Now, Gove had in his workshop, behind
his shop, a Springfield rifle, to which he was putting
new sights. The truth is that every now and then,
some discontented U.S. soldier would desert from
Fort Lyon, or one of the other U.S. forts along the
frontier, often taking with him his excellent breech-
loading Government rifle, made at the U.S. armoury,
Springfield, Mass. This the deserter would promptly
trade off to the first ranchman he could strike a
bargain with, for a suit of civilian clothes, and go
on his way. Often the rancher would prefer
ordinary hunting sights to the Government rifle
sight, and would get a gunsmith to alter them for
him. That was how a Springfield rifle came to
be no very rare object in Gove's workshop. And
on such a rifle was Gove busy one day, when in
came Governor McCook, who wanted something
done to one of his guns. His soldierly eye spotted
the Springfield rifle lying on that work bench in
a moment.

" Hello, Mr. Gove," he burst out, half in earnest,
half jocularly, "that's Government property I see
there. Guess I'll be putting in a claim for that."

"Not by a jugful, you won't," Gove abruptly
flung back at him. " This was put into my hands
by a ranchman, and back into his hands I'll deliver

it. You may be governor of this Territory all right, but you can't seize the property of no private citizen through me."

I forget how they went on, but I know Gove stuck to the Springfield, and the Governor refrained from pushing his demand for it. What did amuse me was the gloriously independent position of the man of the shop, the gunsmith, to the man holding the highest office in the Territory, one appointed by President Grant himself. His standpoint was absolute equality as between man and man. Yes, as a stranger there had already told me : " Denver's the capital of Colorado, and Colorado's the freest country on God's earth."

And when I heard Gove talk so, I began to think it looked like it.

CHAPTER IV

TIGER BILL

THOUGH I was too shy to introduce myself to Governor McCook in Gove's workshop, fortune nevertheless was kind enough to help me in the matter just when I most needed her help, and by good luck I got to know a friend of his. This was a Mr. Matthews, a travelling artist, who was going round the principal towns of the Territory with a panorama of his own painting. He was a quick and clever draughtsman, and he had fixed it up with Governor McCook that he should go down to Los Pinos, where the Governor was to open a new agency for the Southern Utes on the Pacific slope. The scheme was that Matthews should do pictures of him for *Harper's Weekly*. At least he told me it was for Harper's, but of course I could not really say if it mayn't have also been for other illustrated papers. Anyway I feel sure he said Harper's.

"I'll do him up in style," said Mr. Matthews, "do him as the Apostle of Civilization! Oh, I'll give 'em Governor McCook nobly extending the right hand of fellowship to his Red Brethren. Red sons of biscuits I call 'em." He gave a sneering laugh. "But that don't go down with the high-

toned public back East. We're both of us from Ohio, the Governor and me, and I'll show them Eastern ducks Governor McCook inaugurating the new era of peace and goodwill with the savage denizens of the wilderness." He laughed more sneeringly than ever. " Oh, Harper's 'll just ladle it out fine," he said, " and the Governor'll be as pleased as punch ; I've got it fixed up with him so I'll get my pay for the work, and then everybody will be suited all round."

" When are you going ? " said I.

" Why, right away," he answered ; " that is, just as soon's I can get fixed up. I've bought a new 2¾-inch half-spring Schuttler waggon, and I've got to raise the sides a bit so as to take my panorama box in it safely with the camp outfit stowed on top of it. Soon as that's done I'm off."

It didn't take very long for me to arrange to have the honour of accompanying Mr. Matthews. I was to have the privilege of paying him $1 a day and riding on the waggon seat with him and helping him cook and look after the mules and do camp-work generally, and he'd take me to Los Pinos. Thus I should see the whole length of Colorado Terri-tory and make the acquaintance of the Redman at home under the best auspices. Mr. D. A. Cheever, whose kind heart prompted him to look after me like a father and who at first was a little inclined to be distrustful of Mr. Matthews, ended by giving his consent, and Governor Gilpin was glad I was to see the Great Cordillera and that brightest gem of the whole world, the San Luis Park.

" It is," he said, walking up and down the office,

his right hand extended as an orator's, " an immense elliptical basin enveloping the sources of the Rio del Norte. It is isolated in the heart of the continent 1200 miles from any sea. It is mortized, as it were, into the midst of the vast mountain bulk, where, rising gradually from the oceans, the highest amplitude and altitude of the continent is attained."

On he went in this lofty strain for a long time. " The colours," he said, "of the sky and atmosphere are intensely vivid and gorgeous ; the dissolving tints of light and shade are for ever interchanging ; they are as infinite as are the altering angles of the solar rays in his diurnal circuit."

There was plenty more in the same vein. It was highfalutin, but all the same it did thrill me, for, as I said before, he meant it, every word of it. And I have to admit it was true.

And so for the time being I joined my fortunes to those of the peripatetic artist, Mr. Matthews, and when all was at last ready we mounted side by side on the spring seat of the $2\frac{3}{4}$-inch Schuttler waggon behind Sally and Suse, a beautiful pair of sorrel mules—sorrel is the American term for light chestnut in England—and together we set out on our long drive to the San Luis Park and the Los Pinos Agency across the range over on the Gunnison. We made our first camp twenty miles south of Denver at old Dowd's on Cherry Creek.

Dowd's on Cherry Creek was just one of the ordinary wayside stopping-places of which Colorado had any number along the old freighting roads of pre-railroad days : Dowd himself, a cheerful Irish-

man of sixty or so, kept the bar and handed out drinks, while his wife and daughters looked after the cooking and stood ready to dish up the hash for all comers. There were several bull-teams lying there which were coming down from the Divide with lumber (i.e. boards), and these were camped across the road from Dowd's place, and their work-oxen were feeding out somewhere back in the hills. The Divide was the pine-clad watershed between the Platte and the Arkansas. So Matthews and I camped alongside of the bull-whackers and cooked our own hash out of the supplies we carried with us in the waggon ; but after supper we left our camp fire and strolled into the bar to see what might be going on.

We found several bull-whackers inside, as well as a ranchman or two from the neighbourhood —there were ranches all along Cherry Creek—and we passed the time of day with them ; when suddenly the rumble of a waggon outside came to our ears, the next moment the door opened, and four men entered, three of them supporting and indeed half-carrying the fourth, who seemed pretty limp. I took it for a case of a common drunk, but I was wrong ; something had really happened, and all the others, being old hands, spotted the fact long before ever it dawned upon a tenderfoot like myself.

" Hello, Jake," called out Tom Jones, one of the ranchmen, a friendly little chap that I had been talking to, " what's up with Jim ? "

" Got a hole bored in him," returned Jake shortly. " We had a little fun with the police in

there on Larimer Street and Marshal Hopkins plugged him. It was a darned shame of Hopkins. We hadn't done nothing except holler a little and blow off steam, when he shouted to us, and as we didn't stop he jes' pulled his gun and started shooting. We didn't shoot back nor nothing : we hadn't come to Denver for any sech fun, least of all with the police ; but Jim here was plugged, and so we got him round the corner, and away from the police, and back to the Mammoth, shoved him in the waggon and drove out here like hell."

Larimer Street I knew to be a street in Denver, and the Mammoth was a big corral or stopping-place for teamsters and ranchmen when they came to town.

" Is he hurt bad ? " queried Tom Jones.

" Can't say yet," replied Jake. " He don't seem very bad, but we couldn't stop to examine it in Denver and thought we'd best hurry on out here. Turn up that lamp a bit and we'll have a look."

So Jim was laid flat on the bar counter under the smoky petroleum lamp, and deft hands very carefully loosened and opened his clothes. This was all done by the men : Mrs. Dowd and her girls stayed in the kitchen behind the bar-room, and did not come forward as nurses. In those days there were about ten men to one woman in the Territory, and men had to do most things for themselves, nursing included. Jim's shirt being tucked up well above his middle an ominous bluish hole became visible just over the right hip. I stared at it fas-

cinated ; it was the first hole made by a bullet
I ever saw.

" Scott ! " said Tom Jones. " That looks bad !
He's gut-shot, bound to be." In those days, when
antiseptics were but little understood and inocula-
tion against tetanus was unknown, any man shot
through the bowels was doomed to die a painful
and lingering death.

At this Jim, lying there dead still, opened his
mouth ; his eyes were still shut.

" It don't feel like I was gut-shot," he said. " Is
there any of my insides sticking out, as you can see ? "

His voice was low and as cool as if he was dis-
cussing some one else's hurt. I stood amazed.

Tom Jones fingered the skin around the wound,
but did not attempt to probe it. Then his fingers
seemed to follow, as it were, a track right round
to the opposite hip. His eyes had an absorbed
look : clearly he was trying to make his mind
interpret whatever the feel of his fingers told him.
Suddenly he cried out :

" I've got it. It's here, right here over the other
hip just under the skin."

" What's that you say you got ? " queried Jim
in the same cool, low, dispassionate tones.

" The bullet," cried Tom eagerly. " It's lodged
right under the skin and I can feel it. It's a conical,
not a round, bullet. Say, it must have glanced
going in and run right around just under the skin.
I don't believe it's ever got into the hollow of the
man at all."

" Can ye cut it out ? " said Jim.

I was more than ever amazed at his magnificent coolness.

"Who's got a sharp knife?" said Tom with a rapid glance round the company.

No doubt every man there had a knife on him of sorts.

"Best thing's a razor if you got one," commented the imperturbable wounded man.

"I've got a razor," shouted Dowd excitedly. He put his head through the door to the kitchen. "Here you, Dick, girl, where's that razor of mine?" he cried. "Quick with it now."

Dick was his eldest daughter and his wife's chief help in dishing up hash. I was named Dick myself, and it quite startled me thus to hear for the first time my name given to a woman. In another moment Dick burst in with the razor held out in her hand, looking curiously at the patient on the counter, and then even harder at Tom.

"Hand over," said Tom Jones, reaching for it. "Lower that lamp a bit now. Steady on, Jim!"

"Carve away," returned the subject to be operated on. "You carve and I'll grit my teeth and grin."

The very idea of an anæsthetic seemed never to cross the minds of these men. Yet there were surgeons and good ones too—a fact I was fated to find out later—in Denver City.

Bending so as to see as well as possible in that dim light, Tom Jones deftly slit the skin over the hip with the keen razor edge, and next moment the bullet was in his hand. He looked at it knowingly.

" Jes' as I thought," he interjected. " It's a Colt ·44-calibre sharp-pointed bullet. That's why it glanced so easy. I'd have thought Hopkins would have knowed enough to choose a round or a blunt-nose. They ain't so liable to glance off."

A sort of assenting murmur came from the room. Everybody seemed to understand perfectly all about it. Horrible experts these frontiers-men in the business of killing men. Skilful about wounds, though, too. Well, out here they had better be ! They soon mopped up what little blood had come from the place whence Tom Jones had extracted the bullet, put some kind of a pad over both places, that is to say the holes of entrance and exit, and put Jim to bed in one of the sleeping-rooms well away fron the bar. Something was said of taking him to his ranch which lay somewhere up Cherry Creek only a few miles off, but they decided not to carry him a foot farther that night.

Rest was what was needed now.

Matthews and I remained in the bar while the others disposed of the imperturbable Jim, and we now noticed a man lying in a corner of the bar asleep. " Sleeping off his whisky " was my guess, and this time the tenderfoot was not so far out. The man had never stirred from his heavy slumbers during the operation on Jim, but now the sleep seemed to leave him. He opened his eyes, yawned, stretched, and then struggled to his feet ; apparently the result of having slept off a good deal of his load of whisky was that he wanted more, for he said so, and said it with quite superfluous emphasis and profanity.

" Ah, ye don't want any more, Bill," answered
old Dowd soothingly. " Sure ye've had plenty
whisky for to-night. Ye'd better get off to yer
bed, man, and ye'll wake up in the morning feeling fine."

" That I will not," returned the man in a very
surly voice. " I want my drink, and I want
my money out of you, Corny Dowd, and what's
more I'm going to have it." And he hit the bar
with a thump with his huge fist that made the
glasses jump an inch high. He was a big, bearded
man, full six feet tall, with a pair of shoulders on
him like a buffalo bull.

" Ah, Bill, go to bed, now, and be 'asy," said
Dowd, evidently most anxious to pacify him.
" We'll talk about yer pay when morning comes,
and I'll have time to see what there is coming
to ye. These ain't my business hours."

" It's my business hours, though," roared the
man. " You hear me talk. I want my money,
and I'm not a-going to wait for it. Right here and
now's the ticket. Hand over ! You've got the
spondulics right there." He towered over the
bar and the shrinking old man behind it as if he
was going to seize the till. What would happen
if he did, I wondered. The bull-whackers sat
looking on without moving. Would Dowd shoot ?
Would there be a row right here, with ·44-calibre
bullets flying around, and the innocent Mr. Matthews
and myself unwilling spectators, possibly victims.

Instantly the Cheyenne cowboy's phrase about
wanting it " powerful bad " flashed through my

brain. Right here and right now, possibly, was when I wanted it ; but where, oh, where was my beautiful brand-new Colt's Navy pistol ? Safely stowed away in my blankets in the waggon across the road. Not where it should be, ready to my hand just behind my right hip. Of course the quarrel was none of mine, but all the same I'll admit I didn't half like it. Luckily at this instant the door opened, and back came the party of ranchmen, having seen their friend Jim safely tucked up in bed. They seated themselves, as before, on the empty boxes which were the substitute for chairs in Dowd's bar, and stared in silence at the angry giant, who after one glance at them and a moment's pause began again.

" My money," he roared furiously, " my money that's coming to me ! and I'm going to have it ! "

" Looks like he's on a tear," said Tom Jones to me aside in a low voice. " He's Dowd's black-smith, works there for him at the forge across the road. He's done shoeing for me. When he's sober he's a good enough smith. But to-night his whisky seems to have sent him on the war-path, and he ain't called Tiger Bill for nothing."

It certainly did seem as if the whisky had gone right into his brain. Tiger Bill wheeled sharp round from the bar-counter and, facing the room, tore off his coat and tore open the front of his dirty flannel shirt, exposing a huge buffalo-like chest covered with a black mat of hair. He sprang three perpendicular feet aloft in air, clicked both heels together before he hit earth again, threw

both his clenched fists above his head, and yelled :
" I'm a gaulderned son of a biscuit from the
Arkansaw. I run on brass wheels. I'm a full-
breasted roller with three tits. Holes punched for
more ! Now hear me talk ! I'm going to clean
out this gaulderned thieving old son of a biscuit
here who won't pay me my money before you can
say——"

He was interrupted suddenly : there came a
flash of petticoats, and Mrs. Dowd who had been
listening from behind the door to the kitchen darted
into the bar with a feminine screech and set her
ten commandments in his face, dragging her nails
down each cheek.

Tiger Bill hardly seemed to notice beyond pushing her aside with one great arm as easily as if he
were brushing away a feather. All, including the
bull-whackers and Matthews and myself, were on
our feet now, while Bill continued to yell :

" I'll fight any son of a biscuit in this bar—or
any two—or any three ! "

It was a comprehensive challenge, and to my
surprise already, almost before the words were out
of his mouth Tom Jones, who wasn't half the giant's
size, had his coat off.

" I don't care if I take him on, boys," he began.

But the half a dozen bull-whackers and the three
or four ranchmen had closed round Bill, and pushing
aside Mrs. Dowd had got hold of Bill's arms and
crowded him back against the wall. I saw no
blows struck ; they were too quick for him and had
got into too close quarters. It really became a

pushing match, and indeed it looked quite like a football scrum, the way the legs of all those men pushing against Bill made an angle with the floor.

Practically they had got him now so that he couldn't hurt anybody; the crowd wasn't angry with him in point of fact; apparently these bull-whackers had a true fellow-feeling for anyone who had taken more whisky than he could carry; half a dozen voices kept telling him to " dry up " and " quit fussin' when there are ladies round." This fact was undeniable, for Mrs. Dowd and her Dick were still there, eagerly looking on from the door into the kitchen.

Gradually the voices of friendly counsel and the pressure of the men's bodies prevailed; the tightly squeezed giant grew or seemed to grow distinctly less belligerent. Tom Jones put on his coat again. I saw him glance at Dick Dowd as he did, and it dawned on me that he had been ready to fight a man twice his size to please her.

Escorted by the crowd which still pressed tight and close around him, though all went on talking to him in friendly fashion enough, the partially tamed Tiger Bill allowed himself to be taken out through the front door and so across to the forge, where he was induced at last to go to bed, in his own quarters which he had there, and sleep off the rest of his whisky. Then the bull-whackers turned into their blankets beside their waggons drawn up close alongside the forge and said they'd see to it that Bill didn't rampage no more. The first bar-room fuss I ever saw was over, and no harm done.

The ranchmen hitched up their teams and drove off to their ranches. I helped one of the men named Jake to put in his mules.

"Won't be no trouble now," remarked Jake, "leastways I guess not. To-morrow morning Tom Jones and me'll get an order on the Elephant Brewery out of old Dowd for what money there's owing to Bill, and we'll drive Bill straight into Denver and give him his money there and he can turn himself loose as much as he wants to in Denver. Nor I don't care a damn if he does get plugged there. I guess Marshal Hopkins'll attend to him right enough."

"You and Tom Jones seem very willing to take a lot of trouble for old Dowd," I ventured to suggest. "It seems very kind and neighbourly of you both. I've only just come out to this country, you know, but what has struck me most is the way in which people here stand ready to help one another in a difficulty. But of course there may be good reasons for it. It did strike me that Tom Jones looked very hard at Miss Dowd that time he stripped to fight."

Jake laughed.

"Wal', you say as you've only just come out to this new country, but you've learnt to use your eyes some already, if you are a tenderfoot. Yes, we're willing to be as good neighbours as we know how, Tom Jones and me are, to old man Dowd, you can bet your life on that. A man what's got a lot of good-looking dar'ters can most allus find plenty of help handy to drive his cattle for him. So long."

And giving his reins a shake he clucked to his mules, and then as if some thought had come into his mind he checked them again.

" Look at here," he said, " you're a tenderfoot, but you're pretty white, I take it.   Lemme jest drap you a hint.   You've seen this Tiger Bill, as they call him round here.   Wal', you can take it from me he's not quite as tough as he lets on to be.   Too much chin about him, hey ?   You tumble to that ?   Chin-music, I mean.   Gas !   That's all his talk there in the bar amounted to.   Gas !   But now don't you forget it.   There is a Bill down south, where I understand you're going, and you want to look out for him if you run across him.   He's the real Wild Bill from the Arkansaw, and, you hear me, he'll bear watching.   'Nuff said."

He clucked to his mules once more, and this time disappeared in earnest.

Mr. Matthews, as I soon learned, was an extremely early starter, and he and I were off before sun-up next morning ; so I never learned whether Tiger Bill managed to set Denver on fire or whether Tom Jones and Dick Dowd made a match of it ; but I think it more than likely that both arrangements came off.   Anyway I feel perfectly confident of one thing :   the Denver police were abundantly able to take care of Tiger Bill.

CHAPTER V

THE next day Matthews and I crossed the Divide, which rose to about 3000 feet above Denver or some 9000 above sea. Up here was not open grass country but a magnificent forest of Rocky Mountain pines, and here therefore were established several sawmills in full swing, from which came the sawn lumber out of which Denver was built. Roughly, the gradient going up the Divide was about 50 feet to the mile, and I discovered that I was going to have lots of walking exercise on this trip, for every time we came to a hill Matthews would sing out " Chance to walk ! " and I, nothing loath, took the hint, hopped off the spring seat, and hoofed it to the top. If the hill was really steep we both walked.

At the top of the Divide we came into full view of Pike's Peak. I am no hand at describing scenery, but a truly noble mountain it is. The height is something well over 14,000 feet or about 1000 feet lower than Mont Blanc ; the shape distinctly recalled to me the great Monarch of the Alps, but the colour of Pike's Peak is absolutely different. Mont Blanc is intensely white, the pure cold white of the eternal snow ; on Pike's Peak no white

snow can you see in summer, but instead are endless cliffs and gullies of naked granite, all glowing
red, which tower away up into the sky far above
the dark pine-clad ranges at their feet. Here,
distant a good thousand miles and more from any
large body of water, and elevated more than a
mile vertically above sea level, the dry air is crystalline, clear, translucent. Pike's Peak from fifty
miles off seems so close that you might think you
had only to stretch out your hand in order to touch
it ; you feel inclined to say, " I'll just stroll quietly
up there to-morrow morning before breakfast,"
while in the back of your mind you know perfectly
well that a whole week would hardly give you time
enough to get to it and up it.

That is where the mountain magic of the Rockies
lies, in their most thin pellucid air. In Switzerland and other mountain lands the mystery comes
from trailing clouds and streaming mists that
shroud the half-seen, half-hidden peaks at which
you peep only through the veil. Here it is the
amazingly sharp clearness of every detail that
seems beyond belief.

" Gay old Peak," grinned Matthews, " ain't he ?
That's where they found the gold ten years back,
when they started the Pike's Peak or Bust rush
across the Plains. And there was lots of 'em that
did bust, and busted badly too, I reckon. But
there's some left as didn't ; and I guess here's
one of 'em coming to talk to us this blessed minute."

From the direction of Monument Creek a ranchman on a grey horse was loping across the rolling

pasturelands—we were out of the pine forest now —with the evident intention of intercepting us. Matthews pulled up the waggon so as to make it more easy for him.

"I s'pose he's hunting lost horses," he sneered. "Every ranchman in Colorado seems to be allus' in that fix."

Matthews was dead right, as he often was. The rider, a fine stalwart specimen of the frontier ranchman, reined up alongside the waggon, greeted us, and began with some haste :

"Have ye happened to see any stray horses along the road ? "

It came out so slick I nearly laughed aloud.

"No," answered Matthews, "I haven't seen any horses that looked like strays ; I saw a bunch of loose mares and colts about five miles back, but they looked to me to be wonted there."

Animals on their own range take things easier than do strays ; they not only feel at home, but look it, a fact which became familiar enough to me later on.

"Say, what's your brand on them horses, 'case I should run on to 'em lower down the creek ? Mebbe I could send you word back by some one passing."

"Wal'," said the ranchman, "there's different brands on 'em. Mine's T. S. for Tom Summers, that's my name ; but I don't use to put it on a horse that's been branded already : I hate to see a horse with most of the English Alphabet burned into his hide, to say nothing of the map of Mexico."

This was a humorous allusion to the hieroglyphic Mexican brands.

"Why, is your name Summers?" exclaimed Matthews with animation. "I believe it was you I heard a man talking of at old Dowd's on the other side of the Divide and saying you had been one of the crowd that had the big fight with the Cheyennes over on Big Sandy last summer. Billy Wilson's crowd it was, he said, and he told me, too, that you'd had a mighty close call. That so?"

"Yes," assented the other, "you bet your boots it's so, and you're darned well right to say it was a close call. I was right thar', yes, me, looking as I do; and I don't want nuthin' closer. If it hadn't been for Wild Bill, I think likely we'd have all of us bin' lying out thar' now."

"Du tell!" said Matthews. "I'd like well to know the 'hull truth of how it was."

The upshot was that Mr. Summers agreed to tell us more about the big fight if we would come and camp over at his ranch which lay quite near. This, as it was already evening, Matthews agreed to do; while Mr. Summers rode on to have one more try for his strays after having most hospitably invited us to eat and sleep with him; this, however, was an honour which Matthews declined. He was a confirmed dyspeptic and preferred his own private food cooked in his own way; let me add, too, he taught me how to cook a digestible dinner, an accomplishment for which I have reason to be grateful. But after our own supper, and after Sal and Suse, the beautiful mules, of which I was

already growing quite fond, had been fed and picketed we went in to Tom Summers' house to hear his story.

Tom hadn't found his horses yet, but that didn't seem to worry him.

" I'll get 'em to-morrow, likely," was his philo-sophic way of putting it. " I've sure got all the time there is."

Certainly Tom was a man who took his time about things, and I had better condense his long story here considerably. It seemed that in 1863 a regiment of Colorado Volunteers fell on a Camp of Cheyennes on Big Sandy Creek where they slew a good many of them. The men who did the slay-ing were men who had suffered from the awful atrocities of the outbreak of the Plains Indians in that year. I have since come across other Colorado men who took the view that these parti-cular Cheyennes had already come in and reported themselves to the general commanding at Fort Lyon, as willing to surrender, and that he, not having food for them, had sent them out to kill buffalo on Big Sandy, and that therefore they should have been let alone. However that may be (and I dare say Coloradans argue over it yet), five years later, that is to say in the summer before I arrived in Colorado, a very strong war-party of Cheyenne braves had come to Big Sandy and held a war dance there, and then attacked the scattered ranches all the way from the Divide to the Fountain River. Immediately a ranchman named Billy Wilson raised a party (forty or fifty strong, I think

Tom said) and followed hard after them, caught them on the head of Big Sandy, or somewhere at any rate south and east of Bijou Basin, and gave battle. Unfortunately the Indians were far more numerous and proved only too willing to take the Wilson crowd on. They got completely round the white men and killed some of them and practically all their riding stock ; so that Wilson and his party were brought to bay behind a barricade of dead horses, where they desperately resolved to make their last stand. If the Indians charged home the white men would sell their lives dear ; but remembering the torture they did not intend to be taken alive ; each man swore he was going to keep his last bullet for himself. But the Indians, past-masters in this sort of warfare, and well knowing that they had their enemies corralled, declined to charge home on desperate men, and contented themselves with cunningly lying down all round them under safe cover. In this way they would force the whites ultimately to come out and expose themselves to be shot if they did not want to die of hunger and thirst. An appalling end seemed to be close at hand for the whole party, and they realized that their one chance was for some man either to ride or creep out through the Indian line under cover of night and take the news swiftly to the settlements and bring up a fresh band of Indian fighters to their relief. The first man who volunteered for this service was Wild Bill.

"No, not your friend, Tiger Bill," said Summers,

in answer to my eager question as to whether it
was the would-be desperado whom I had just
told him Matthews and I had been seeing at old
Dowd's. "Nor it ain't Bill Hickok; he's another
Wild Bill they've got over there in Kansas, and a
mighty fine man too, so they say; but he don't
live here in Colorado. This Wild Bill of ours lives
down here on the Arkansaw mostly, or on the
Fountain or thereabouts; he works on a ranch
usually, or at any job he can get. He's called
Wild Bill for several things he's done, including
killing various men at various times. But I've
always understood as the most of 'em was men that
wanted killing."

"Men who wanted it like our friend, Tiger Bill,
over at old Dowd's?" I ventured.

"P'r'aps so," assented Summers. "Anyway, Wild
Bill was well known for a desperate character, a
man who took chances; and we all agreed that
if there was anybody likely to get through it was
him. He should have the first chance to see what
he could do. What he quite declined to do, however, was to try to creep on foot through the Injuns.
'To begin with, they're bound to get me if I try
that,' sez he, 'and then if they was to take me alive
they'd sure put me to the torture. Trust Injuns
for that. No, what I want is as you should tie
me on to Billy Wilson's race-horse, and I'll go
through 'em a-whoopin'. If I'm tied on, even if
they do hit me, the horse might carry me through
unless they plugged him too; and I might make
it back to the settlements so, even with one or

two holes bored in me.   Now, afoot I couldn't expect to do that.'

" We all saw that there was sense in what Bill said, horse-sense as you might call it in every sense of the word.   Also we felt that Bill was less likely to be taken alive for the torture that way.   So we done exactly as Wild Bill said.   We took Bob Lee, that was an A number 1 racehorse Billy Wilson had along that he rode, and by good luck the horse hadn't been hit.   The way Wilson saved him when the rest of the horses was killed was this.   He had trained him to lie down at the word, and when the Injuns corralled us Wilson made Bob Lee lie down, and there he lay exactly like a dead horse, same as the others.   But, when night came, we got him on to his feet and rubbed his legs good to get the stiffness out, and we tied Bill on to his bare back, good and fast, with two guns belted on him. It was plumb dark ; there was no moon ; and so in the dark away went Bill, lickety split, right through the line of them Injuns.   'Course they fired at him a-plenty, and though we couldn't see neither Bill nor the Injuns, yet we see the flash of the shots right enough, and we fired a lot of shots ourselves —not in Bill's direction, you understand—so as to confuse them a bit.   But we couldn't tell if they'd got him or if he'd got away clear.   They yelled a-plenty, but that didn't tell us nuthin' ; Injuns was bound to yell anyhow.   After a while things quieted down, and we laid still, wondering if we'd live to see another day or lose our scalps to them sons of guns.   And then dawn come, and we

listened, and heard nuthin'; and we looked, and we saw nuthin'; and then we crept out of our holes that we'd dug ourselves to lie in in the sand with our knives, and, you better believe, thar' warn't an Injun anywhere around. Bill had got clean away, and they, knowing he'd bring rein-forcements, had just quietly vamoosed in the night. So we hoofed it home, feeling pretty sick at the loss of our horses, and of some friends, but mighty glad to be alive at all, which was more than we'd expected the night before."

"And Wild Bill?" I asked.

"Oh, he was all right," answered Tom. "Their bullets never tetched him. He got away, and was raisin' a fresh party for to relieve us when we got back to the settlements. What's become of him, you ask? Oh, I believe he's working on a ranch or something somewheres down on the Arkansaw. If you was to come acrost him as you're going that way (Matthews had mentioned that we were making for Cañon City, which is on the Arkansaw), you can tell him from me that he can be sure of getting a job up this way any time he wants it. Bill's a man, let me tell you, that's not always easy to get along with, but we here up around the Divide ain't forgot what he did that time. Why ain't he easy to get along with, you say? Wal', some folks says he's mad. He takes notions into his head, and he's mighty sudden in bringing of 'em out sometimes. He's startling, that's about the size of it; but when a man's killed several men already it's kind of trying to the nerves to have

him startle you.   You'll see what I mean in a holy minute if you ever meet him."

At this point I may interrupt myself to explain that Billy Wilson was able to raise that crowd to fight Indians because he was a man well known for his courage and skill.   Billy certainly was a rare good plucked one.   Four years later, in 1873, I saw him strap himself on to the back of an ill-tempered race-pony owned by Tom Russell and myself, and I wondered then did he give a thought to the time when he had helped to strap Wild Bill on to Bob Lee.   Billy strapped himself on to our evil-tempered race-pony Charmer in order to ride him in a race, because the pony, a cream-coloured quarter-horse from Oregon, when first mounted, had thrown and hurt badly Garcia, a splendid Mexican rider whom we had put up.   But this, as I say, was four years later, and not even in my dreams of 1869 did I have the faintest forecasting of it.

Just now what I was eager for was to hear more of the fighting and in particular to know how these frontiers-men played the game of war.

" Of course you must have killed some of the Indians," was my diplomatic way of putting it, " that is when you were fighting them, I mean. Did you scalp them ?   Have you got a real genuine scalp ?   I'd most truly like to see one."

It was thrilling to feel oneself so close to a desperate struggle of only a year ago and to be in the actual presence of one of the brave survivors of the fighting.

Mr. Summers smiled at my eagerness.

" No," he said rather grimly, " I hain't no scalps.
I don't hold much with scalping. Leave that
to the redskins, says I. No self-respecting white
man didn't ought to lower himself like that : why it's
coming down to their level, that's what I call it."

" I thought you told me that white men out
here took scalps ? " said I, turning to Matthews.
" I thought you said they stuck at nothing, not
even at eating human flesh sometimes, didn't
you ? "

I had listened to a good many of Matthews'
yarns along the road. He, as I should have explained,
being from Ohio, a Western State, called himself
a Western man. But he declined to be classed as
a Far Western tough, and I had heard him say some
pretty strong things about the " hard citizens "
(that was a great phrase of his) living out on the
frontier. He glanced deprecatingly now at Tom.

" Oh, well," he said, " one gets to yarning, and
anyhow it takes all sorts to make a world. No, I
don't deny I said there were some pretty tough men
out on the frontier who stuck at nothing. But
you've got hold of the wrong end of the stick,
Mr. Townshend. I never said as everybody out on
the frontier was tough, not by no manner of means.
There's just as high-toned people here as anywheres
else. And don't you forget it."

Evidently he was anxious to propitiate Mr.
Summers. But my appetite for horrors had been
whetted, and besides I did not particularly enjoy
being sat upon like that by Mr. Matthews. I was
under no obligation to him ; indeed it was decidedly

the other way about : I was doing half the work as well as paying him $30 a month for the trip. So I stuck to my point. " Don't you remember, Mr. Matthews," I persisted, " how you yourself told me about Liver-eating Johnson only yesterday ? That's what I was referring to."

It was a peculiarly horrible tale that had been the worst of a whole string of Western stories which Matthews had poured into my too willing ears.

" Oh, that ! " he said. " That was entirely exceptional : a case by itself, absolutely ! "

Evidently he wanted to pass it off. But by this time Mr. Summers had been aroused to take a definite interest.

" What was that ? " he asked. " I never heard tell of any Liver-eating Johnson. Who was he ? "

Thus pestered, Matthews had to explain ; while as for me I was nothing loath to hear the whole story over again.

" It was 'way off in Wyoming," began Matthews, " beyond Laramie Plains up near South Pass. There was a man there called Johnson who had a woman living with him ; indeed, I rather think that he called her his wife. And one day an Indian came along and insulted her, a Blackfoot or a Sioux, I'm not rightly sure which. And she complained to Johnson about it when he come home. And he was mad, fair mad, Johnson was. He just swore, then and there, that he'd get on that Indian's trail till he caught him, and that when he caught him he'd eat his liver. Yes, he got really quite

mad over his woman having been insulted. And he was a man who generally did what he said too. He hunted that Indian, and caught him, and cut his liver out, and fried it, and eat it. So up there they all called him Liver-eating Johnson, naturally."

"First I ever heard of it," said Tom Summers in non-committal tones. "However, it's a long ride from here to South Pass, and I don't know but the thing might be true. But it ain't usual. And I never saw any man myself as I think would have done it. As a rule we white men don't care to lower ourselves so."

It was pretty plain that while Mr. Summers didn't want flatly to contradict Matthews, he also didn't more than half-believe the story, and was very distinctly jealous for the reputation of the frontier. I had to respect him both for his politeness and his honourable repudiation of such brutality as characteristic of his fellow frontiers-men. And I will say here that Mr. Liver-eating Johnson, if he ever really existed, was most certainly an exception, and ten years of frontier life, in my case, did but confirm Mr. Summers' attitude.

Matthews and I retired to our blankets beside the waggon and rolled out next morning early before sun-up, while Mr. Summers, I presume, returned to his usual routine of hunting for those lost horses.

As Mr. Summers had anticipated, so the thing turned out : we did come across the real Colorado Wild Bill himself down on the Arkansaw at Cañon City. It took some three days' travel for us, keeping that great red dome of Pike's Peak always to our

right, to get down to the Fountain River, cross it
and travel on and up over some low Divides till
we reached the point where the Arkansaw emerges
from its cañon and comes out of the mountains
on to the Plains.   Here stands Cañon City, its name
clearly taken from its position.   A toll-road ran
from here away off into the mountains to South
Park, and it was by this road that Matthews proposed to travel.   Also he proposed to rest his mules
at Cañon City for a day and exhibit his show.   Mr.
Matthews, the travelling artist, was in point of fact
a showman.   We put up at a little rough hotel
kept by a Mr. Helm and his wife, and Tommy their
twelve-year-old boy was most eager to help over
setting up the Grand Rocky Mountains Panorama,
which constituted the show, in a hall which Matthews
hired.   Help was needed to get the heavy coffin-
like box out of the waggon as well as for setting
it up in the hall.   Helm found Matthews a couple
of men to assist, and Tommy, the boy, explained
to me in an excited undertone that one of them was
Wild Bill.   " Oh, he's killed a lot of men," he said.
That was what fetched the boy's imagination.

It fetched mine too, I will admit.   Of course I
gladly lent a hand in the awkward job of unloading
the giant's coffin, as I called the big box, and taking
it into the hall, but I could not help having one
eye on Wild Bill all the time.   After half a century
one's memory is apt to become a trifle dull, and I
guess I could hardly swear to him to-day if it were
possible for me to run against him, but by my
recollection he was a man rather small than large,

and rather dark than fair. Quite unlike Buffalo Bill, and not less unlike his other great namesake the famous Kansas Wild Bill, Bill Hickok. Also I noticed, not without a little surprise, that if I had my eye on Bill, he likewise had his on me. I noticed, too, that Bill's eye seemed to be particularly attracted by my right hip. The fact was that I was wearing slung to that hip the ·36 Colt's navy pistol which I had bought from Carlos Gove back there in Denver. Remembering that decidedly unpleasant night's experience with Tiger Bill in old Dowd's bar, when I had thought I might want it " powerful bad," and the pistol was not on me but in my blankets across the road, I had decided that in future I would go heeled.

Although Bill, the Manslayer, wore no pistol, or none that my eyes could see, he kept so steadily looking at me that in my innocence I had to wonder what the attraction could be. However, I didn't care enough about it to ask him ; what I wanted to do was to give him Tom Summers' message ; so as soon as opportunity served during the process of setting up the Panorama I spoke to Bill and told him of our meeting with Tom Summers, and told him what Tom had said about him. Bill was mightily pleased to hear it. In a moment he became most friendly and most warmly thanked me for giving him the message.

" Mr. Summers is a mighty white man," he said, " and if you should ever see him again you can tell him that from me. I'm obliged to him, and I'd be well satisfied to go to work up that 'ar way.

But . . . wal', there's some things as keeps me round here." He broke off quite abruptly, nor did he seem to expect me to ask why. But the angry flash in his eye gave me the answer for which I did not dare to ask. Bill's secret was that there was a woman in the case.

"See here," he began again, "I wants to say sum'mat to you that's for your good, if so be you wants to hear it." I nodded assent. "Nor I don't want to say it out right here before everybody ; I was a-goin' to, but I've kind a-changed my mind. How'd you like to come into that room yonder and hear me talk ? " He pointed to a sort of room or office opening off the end of the hall.

"Right you are," said I, " come along."

I led the way in, and he following me turned quick, and with a snap he locked the door behind us. That was startling ; and there came on me like a flash Mr. Summers' remark that Bill had an odd little trick of startling people. But I can't say I liked being startled.

"Now," said Bill, " what d'you carry that gun for you've got slung to your tail ? " He used a coarser word.

"Why," said I, " to defend myself with, I suppose. I certainly want to keep out of trouble."

"And," he cut in, " you're going the very shortest way to get into it. S'pose some feller was to come along and tell you to put away that thing, what'd you do ? "

"Oh," said I, " I suppose I should tell him to go and be blowed."

" And s'posing he didn't go and be blowed,"
returned Bill. " S'posing he got the drop. Where'd
you be then ? "

" I don't quite follow," said I. " What's the
drop ? " though even as I spoke I half guessed.

" What's the drop ? " said Bill, and his lips
twisted themselves into the very grimmest smile
I ever saw on face of man. " Wal', you are a
tenderfoot ! "

He paused and looked me up and down as if to
measure the extent of my greenness. Then dropping
the contemptuous attitude he suddenly said :

" But I'm mighty obliged to you for bringing
that message, I am so ! Yes, sir, I am so. Look
at here ; I reckon I'll be a friend to you, you understand ? Got that right ? "

" Yes," I returned a little doubtfully. I was
glad to have friends in this new country, yet this
man-killing Wild Bill was a queer sort of friend.
But already it had dawned on me that some of
the men I had met out here on the frontier who had
been most friendly to me were—well, not exactly
the " high-tonedest," so to speak.

" I could show you something," Bill went on.
" But I want to be sure you understand as I'm your
friend. Even if I did a little play actin', you understand." If Bill was mad there was method in his
madness.

" Oh, perfectly so," I rejoined readily. " I'm
out to learn. Fire away."

My words were taken more literally than I had
imagined. Like a flash Bill's right hand went

back to his hip, something clicked, and I was looking in the face of a bull-dog revolver at full cock and
pointed straight at me. My hand instinctively
began to move towards my pistol. Quick as thought
came the sharp command: "Don't you touch it.
Don't you dare try to pull that gun, or I'll blow
you through."

I stood rigid: that cocked pistol a yard away
was compelling; so were the flashing eyes in the
cruel hard face behind it.

For seconds which seemed like centuries we
stood motionless, so.

Suddenly Bill dropped his hand, and uncocking
his pistol shoved it behind him.

"Play actin'! Play actin'!" he laughed, but in
a strained way. There was high nervous tension
in his voice, and I instantly remembered how
Summers had said that some men swore he was
mad. Now I knew it. "Now you know what the
drop is," said Bill. "But it was I that had it.
Where was you?"

Well, it was pretty obvious. I was had on toast
—absolutely. Had the affair been in earnest I'd
be the dead man now, and Bill, with the drop,
would be all alive and kicking still. Yes, there
was absolutely no possibility of doubting it. I had
seen the magic of the drop.

"Now, pard," said Bill, dropping into a friendly
confidential tone, "I've showed you what I meant.
A gun like yours is all right riding out on the range.
But if you go around these yer' frontier towns with
it slung to your tail, it's a kind of a challenge, and

some feller's liable to take you on sudden and make you look a fool. That's why I showed it you in here, and locked that door. I didn't want to do it before them others. But you hear me talk. You put that gun away in your blankets ; it's right enough for the road ; but in a place like this, if you want to pack a gun around, put it somewheres where folks can't see it. 'Nuff said."

He unlocked the door, and next moment we were outside again. As my startled wits began to return to me I managed to stammer out something to say that I was grateful ; for in spite of being rather upset I most truly was grateful. I had had a valuable lesson.

The magic of the drop. Alas, poor Bill! I never saw him again, but I heard of his finish three years later when I was ranching on Black Squirrel Creek. This was the story as it reached me.

Bill was working for Mr. John Jones, a married man, and one day when Mr. Jones came home Mrs. Jones complained to him that Bill had insulted her. Mr. Jones was a resolute man ; he went straight to where Bill was, said not a word, but pulled his gun, and got the drop. Bill, recognizing the magic of the drop, knew the uselessness of trying to reach for his gun, and instead tore open the front of his shirt with both hands showing his bare breast over his beating heart. "Shoot, shoot," he cried. It was an off chance. They do say that some men have found themselves unable to shoot thus into a naked breast ; but Mr. Jones was not

one of them ; the next second his bullet was through Bill's heart.

The jury cleared Mr. John Jones. When there was a woman in the case a Colorado jury in those days would clear almost anybody. But I could not help feeling sorry for Bill ; I will add though that once, a year after Bill's death, I had a brief interview with Mr. Jones over a cow (not a cow of mine nor claimed by me) which he asserted his right to, and I did then find him a distinctly unpleasant customer. But I should have to admit that he was probably right over the cow, so possibly he may have been right over Bill. Anyway, he understood only too well the magic of the drop.

CHAPTER VI

OUR RED BROTHERS

FROM Cañon City we plunged into the mountains, and a wonderful journey we had over the old toll-road ; a rocky road it was and no mistake, but Matthews could drive and the mules were staunch and we did get up and down some awful hills. But to ease the work Matthews left his panorama in its huge coffin-like box at a little mountain town, and thus lightened we reached at last the summit of the Poncho Pass between the valley of the Arkansaw and the San Luis Park.

Here we had an interesting meeting. Three men were coming out of the wild mountains off beyond the Park to the west where they had been looking for gold. The three were Dick Irwin, a well-known prospector whom Matthews had met before, and two others. Of course I knew none of them, but Dick and Matthews started off nineteen to the dozen, for the three told us we were the first white men they had seen after coming out of the wild. Naturally the first thing Matthews wanted to know was how much gold they had found, but to this the reply was guarded. Dick hadn't discovered any gulch mines that amounted to anything. He had got a lot of specimens, however,

in the packs, but how much these would prove to be worth he couldn't say, not till they had been submitted to the tests of the assayer. He was guardedly hopeful.

"I'll tell you what we have found, though," said Dick, "and that's the place where Fremont's men eat each other."

"Fremont!" sneered Matthews. "That's the man they call 'the Pathfinder,' who was always lost."

"Wal', he got lost that journey sure," said Dick, "but I dunno as it was his fault. Ef he'd only 'a' had Kit Carson for a guide instead of Bill Williams it might have been all right. 'Twas Bill Williams what lost 'em, and 'twas Bill Williams who started eating the dead ones when they got to starving."

"When was all this?" I inquired eagerly.

"Oh, matter of twenty years back," answered Dick carelessly. "It's an old story now, but it's gone the round of all the camps, you bet. It was a fool trick of General Fremont to try to cross this main range in mid-winter; they did just get across and a blizzard caught 'em and every last one of their mules froze to death, and most of the men too."

"And you've seen the place?" I inquired.

"Yes," he said, "it's over west here and a bit north from the headwaters of the Del Norte. It's a pretty tough country to get through even in summer, and what it must have been like in winter——" He broke off abruptly, leaving our imagination to fill in the details.

" I say," said I, " is that the country where Major Powell's lost himself now, at least so they say in Denver ? "

" Major Powell," echoed Dick. " He's the man who wants to explore the Grand Cañon, isn't he ? No, he'd more likely be farther south and lower down."

" You haven't heard anything of him ? " I queried, mindful of Governor Gilpin's injunction. " Didn't even the Indians know anything about him ? "

" We didn't have much talk with the Injuns," said Dick with a grim smile, " nor we didn't want to. The Utes don't have much use for prospectors over there across the range, and we jes' kept clear of 'em, best we knew how."

" Why, we're going right in there now," returned Matthews. " I'm going to do pictures of Governor McCook at Los Pinos embracing his Red Brethren, and the Triumph of Peace, and that sort of kid-glove stuff." He grinned again in that sardonic way he had, for his bitter jests included himself more often than not.

" Wal', you'd best keep one eye on your pictures," said Dick, " and t'other one on the Utes : they'll bear watching. Them Uncompagres especially : they're terrors."

" They may have killed Powell perhaps," I ventured.

" Likely they have," assented Dick. " Of course I hope they haven't. But as I told you jes' now, I hain't seen nor heard a single thing about him."

And so we parted from Dick, and drove on down

into the glorious San Luis Park. And a wonder it truly was with its ring of huge mountains round it as Governor Gilpin had said, and a precious long drive we had across it to Kerber Creek, where we camped, and from there on to Saguache, a tiny settlement of half a dozen houses, Mexican and American, just where the Saguache Creek emerged from the western mountains. We camped by permission in an outhouse belonging to one Godfrey, an old fur-trader of French-American stock, who was married to a woman half Mexican half Ute. Godfrey himself was absent, having gone on with Governor McCook up the Saguache Creek towards the Cochetopa pass, *en route* for Los Pinos.

Scott ! but I did sleep after that long drive across the Park to Saguache. And then in the middle of the night I was waked by Matthews' hand roughly shaking my shoulder.

" What is it ? " said I, still half-dazed. " Indians about ? " Now that we were really in the vicinity of wild Red Indians my subconscious self was exciting itself over the novel idea.

" Indians, your grandmother ! " came Matthews' contemptuous voice in reply. " No, it's a half-breed baby that's going to croak, and the women think you might be able to do something for it."

" Me ? " said I, sitting up and trying to rub the sleep out of my eyes ; " but I'm not a doctor. I shouldn't know what to do."

" Didn't they learn you anything of any use back there at Cambridge College ? " retorted Matthews with his usual sneer. " Rouse up. You

got to come and squint at the poor little devil just to ease the minds of these Mexican women."

Unwillingly I crawled out of my snug blankets and followed him out into the night, and then into a room in the house, where by the light of a tallow dip I saw two swarthy women bending over an infant's cot. Last night I had hardly noticed them I was so tired; swarthy they were, about like a dark type of Italian: the good old Bible phrase " dark but comely " came into my mind as fitting them exactly. As for the poor baby, the pale hue of death was already in its face plain to see.

I looked at it while they watched me eagerly, but ignorant of medicine what could I do? and presently I beat a retreat. Almost as I did so a horse's steps were heard outside and a man sprang into the room. It was Godfrey himself. He glanced hastily at his dying child. " I'd got to come back," he said. " I've seen the Governor as far as the foot of the Pass, and then I hit out straight for home."

The women murmured something to him in Spanish and he looked over at me.

" Thank 'ee, pard," he said, " you done all you could, I reckon;" and as he turned again to the mother Matthews and I slipped out. The father had arrived just in time to witness his poor little child's death and to do what he might to console the weeping mother.

A few minutes after, Godfrey joined us.

" That's over," he said briefly, " and I've got to

give you the Governor's message, Mr. Matthews.
He wants you to hurry up and join him. We've
managed to get his sawmill outfit over the Pass
and on down to Los Pinos, but the Governor's
waiting for Curtis, the interpreter. He can't hold
his grand pow-wow with them Utes without Curtis,
and he's powerfully uneasy ; the Utes are getting
uglier every day. If you roll out right away now,
before sun-up, you may catch him by noon ; you'll
be safest with him, not that he's what I'd call safe,
not by no manner of means."

Godfrey had the frontiers-man's deep distrust
of " blanket " or wild Indians—a distrust too often
well grounded.

"Oh, shucks ! " cried Matthews. " These Southern
Utes ain't going to make trouble. It's nothing but
chin-music with them. Ouray'll keep 'em quiet."

"Who is Ouray ? " asked I.

"The big peace-chief of the whole Ute nation.
He's not here ; he's off somewheres else just now, but
he's an Indian with brains, and he's been to Washington and seen Uncle Sam's soldiers and rifles and
cannons. He knows. When the Southern Utes
kicked against the treaty he made three years back
ceding to us the whole of the Wet Mountain Valley,
he told Chief Ignacio and the rest of 'em straight
out, ' My beloved brethren, it's no use your kicking ; the white man has a gun for every tree.' Oh,
his head's level. He'll hold 'em down right enough,
whatever old thing the Governor wants out of
'em."

"Maybe so," said Godfrey doubtfully. " I dunno.

But Governor McCook's got a good nerve. Here he is goin' in with his triflin' ten-soldier-man escort when he ought to have a whole regiment of U.S. cavalry with him. He's got this new treaty of his out of Ouray for surrendering the whole Atlantic Slope, that's all of Colorado this side of the Great Divide, and he's to start a new agency for the Southern Utes over at Los Pinos. Now, them wild Utes from far out on the Uncompagre, 'way over on the Pacific Slope, ain't never seen a white man, without it's some unlucky prospector they've scalped ; if they kick now, they and Mr. Shawano have jest exactly got the Governor in the hollow of their hand."

" Who is Shawano ? " I asked.

" Their head war-chief. Ouray's jest their head peace-chief ; he may do the talkee-talkee business with the Government, but Shawano's their real big man. He's a man-killer. He's killed more men than any other Ute, and they jest worship him, and he's got eight hundred warriors there."

With Godfrey's help we hitched up the waggon, and, whipping up the mules, splashed through the first ford of the Saguache Creek. There was no difficulty in following the trail to Cochetopa Pass. The waggons on ahead with the sawmill outfit had left their mark plain enough, and we followed their tracks right to the Governor's camp. We found him fairly snorting with rage. Curtis, the interpreter, had not turned up, and the Governor was in a fix. He was bound to have a reliable interpreter so that no mistakes could be made. In Colorado

in 1869 only two white men spoke Ute. Curtis
was one ; the other was Major Oakes, three hundred
miles away on the Platte. Curtis' absence was no
fault of ours, however, and the General made us
welcome, he and his tiny retinue of Boys in Blue.

And then suddenly there came a white horse
ridden at speed through the timber from the west,
and his rider was an officer in army blue, who sprang
to the ground and saluted.

" General, there's trouble. The Uncompagres
have sworn by all their gods they won't give way.
Ouray hasn't enough backing. There was only
one chief in the lot that had nerve enough to back
him, and I've just passed him sitting alone by
himself on the trail. Kaniatche his name is. He's
got no horse with him. They've set him afoot !
He, a big Ute chief, and afoot ! I couldn't talk
to him, but he made signs to me that the others
had run him out. At least, that's what I guessed."

" And I guess," said the General, " that what
I need is to have a talk with this Mr. Kaniatche
right away. So, Captain Alexander, if, as you say,
he's afoot, you'd better take one of the escort and
a spare horse and fetch him on here as quick as you
can."

An hour later a dignified Red Man was seated
by the camp-fire with his blanket folded majestic-
ally round him. Indian-like, his face indeed was
controlled so as to show no emotion, but his expression was set and solemn. Evidently he had something serious to tell. Oh, if he could only have
put it into English for us ! He did try to explain

in the sign-language, but not one of us could make out much more from that than Captain Alexander had been able to.

" Great Scott ! " groaned McCook, " that interpreter Curtis has fairly put me in a cleft stick. Say, Mr. Matthews, don't you know any squaw-man in these parts who would do instead ? "

A man married to a squaw becomes an interpreter of sorts, for he is bound to find out what his spouse has to tell him, one way or another.

" There's Godfrey's wife, General," said Matthews. " She's half-Ute, at any rate, and I know she understands a lot of their lingo. She's your only chance I can think of round here."

" She's a woman," said the General, " and the Utes are warriors and despise women. And she's got a sick kid ; that was Godfrey's excuse for leaving me here last night."

" Kid's dead," said Matthews.

" That so ? " said the General. " Well, I—I hate to fetch in a woman, but I don't see anything else for it, the way things are. Wonder if she'd leave the grave ? Well, anyway, we must try. Mr. Matthews, would you do me the favour to take my buggy and drive down there as hard as you can, and don't come back without the woman and Godfrey. Say they've got to come."

Matthews hesitated. " Godfrey's mighty independent, General. Will he come when I bid him ? And will he be willing to bring his wife into danger just because you say so ? But it's you that are bossing this show, Governor, and whatever you say goes."

So Matthews departed in quest of the Godfreys ; we could but wait as patiently as we might for his return with them.

Darkness had not long fallen when they reached the camp, and Mrs. Godfrey, as we all called her, proved to know Ute enough to interpret what Kaniatche had to tell.   The General was so impatient to hear it that he hardly gave her time to take supper.

It made a picturesque scene there in the firelight : the dignified Red Man explaining his wrongs, and the eager, absorbed face of the beautiful woman as she leant forward, her shawl drawn over her head, listening to every word.   She told it all in Spanish to Godfrey, and then he in his turn translated it to us.

Kaniatche's tale was simple : he alone among the Southern Utes trusted in the wisdom of Ouray, and was willing to do as the white man wished. For this his brothers had turned on him and driven him forth an outcast.   Therefore he had sought the camp of the great Governor.

The General listened, grimly attentive.   " You come right along with me," he said, when the chief had finished, " to Los Pinos.   I'll see that you're not molested.   The arm of the Great Father at Washington is long enough to protect you."   And the marvel of it was that Kaniatche believed him and consented.

With a courtly bow the General turned to the woman, who was only a half-bred Ute.   " Madam," he said, " you are the one person that has saved the

situation, and I thank you in the name of the United States. You will not, I am sure, refuse to go with us to the end, and see the thing through. Thank you once more." Again his doffed hat swept the ground as with another courtly bow he assumed her consent.

Her eyes were wet ; something was still tugging at her heart-strings, something that pulled her back to her dead baby's grave. Yet she nodded assent.

Then the General gave orders.

" We start at daylight," he said. " One of you boys'll have to give Kaniatche his horse and ride in the cook's waggon instead."

And so next day we reached Los Pinos. The new agency was in a lovely natural park on the Gunnison, and the first frosts had painted yellow and scarlet the quakenasp and dwarf oak that grew thick along the gulches. Every hill-top was crowned with the tall red-stemmed columns of the pines, while the rich bunch-grass clothed all the slopes. The cone-shaped tepees of the Utes stood in clusters, each band grouped, as its sub-chief chose, near wood and water. Naked Indian boys were driving wiry ponies back and forth through the grass, while other boys were coming up from the creek with strings of splendid trout, and the gaily-dressed bucks rode in from the hills with drip-ping red lumps of fresh-killed venison and elk-meat hanging to their saddles. There were enough of them. The sawmill men swore they had counted five hundred tepees, and every frontiers-man knows each tepee counts for at least two warriors.

The new agency was being built in the very middle of the park, and here the sawmill had been started, and the waggons set to hauling in logs to be sawn into timber to build with. This was the true sign of the white man's foot. Already mutilated tree-stumps stood where noble pines had been, yellow sawdust floated down the clear stream —the sawdust that kills the trout—and raw yellow skeleton buildings of unseasoned boards were being hammered together by clattering carpenters. No wonder the wild Uncompagres felt the desecration and shouted for war. Yet even over the wild Indians who had never before seen a white man the General's word had power. He summoned the reluctant chiefs to council, and they came. The debate was long and fierce, for the mountain warriors were stubborn. I looked at the ring of savage faces, and it seemed certain that they would never yield. What were the feelings of the woman who sat there interpreting their threats to the General and giving back his diplomatic answers to the savages in their own tongue ? To have a woman so much as come into council with warriors was gall to the proud Utes. Did her heart quake ? Well she knew how the Utes held us all in the hollow of their hand ; and she knew, too, what her fate would be if they captured her. The Utes spare no horror to their captives. Her husband might keep his last bullet for himself. Would he keep the last but one for her ? Perhaps it was well that her baby was safe in its little grave !

But if these were her thoughts, the Indian blood

in her enabled her to keep them well concealed.
To and fro the tide of argument flowed. When the
Uncompagres grew too insolent, and threatened
us openly, the General answered :

" You may kill me and my ten men, but there
are ten thousand more behind us, and ten times ten
thousand behind them. Ouray has seen them.
Ask him."

The General's confidence in Ouray, publicly
testified, carried weight ; the Uncompagres listened,
and at last they gave way. They would accept
the treaty, and they would receive Kaniatche
back ; the pipe of peace was passed round, and we
all breathed freely again. But the sawmill men,
with the Western man's curious way of taking the
gloomiest view of the future (and yet going on
with the job), swore that, for all their talk of peace,
our lives were not worth an hour's purchase.

When the council broke up and the Indians
returned to their tepees we sought our tents, and
presently a message came from the Ute chiefs that,
as all was settled and peace was now secure, Shawano
himself would give us a grand display of his warriors
in full array. It was noon, and I noticed that
the Indian visitors who had hung about our camp
disappeared. We had just eaten our midday meal,
when the cry was raised, " Here they come ! "
and, running out, Matthews and I beheld, half a
mile off, a long, long line of Indian warriors riding
towards us at a gallop. Out they dashed fully
eight hundred strong from the timber, where they
had evidently been gathering, into the open park,

their gleaming guns in their hands, their faces black with war-paint, their naked bronze bodies shining in the bright sun, the feathers in their long hair dancing behind them in the breeze. Shawano himself in all his glory led them, his gorgeous war-bonnet of eagle-plumes streaming out four feet behind him. To right, to left, he circled in swinging curves, the endless line of warriors following him ; then as if by magic he sent separate bands flying this way and that, forwards and backwards, weaving a maze of figures like a dance. And every man of the eight hundred as he raced along seemed to be a part of his pony, whose swift-twinkling hoofs bore him hither and thither as though man and horse were one.

" I never saw cavalry do evolutions better," said the General, eyeing them intently, his big, burly form a yard or two in advance of the rest of us, with Godfrey and his wife close up behind. Her lips looked drawn with the tense strain of that anxious morning, but her eyes were soft ; she was remembering her baby.

" How in the world does Shawano manage it, General ? " asked Captain Alexander. " He doesn't shout, and he doesn't use a bugle. Yet they all know exactly what he means."

" You've got me there," answered the General. " It's A number 1 ; but the way he does it beats me."

Nearer to us in the plain scoured the flying waves of horsemen, and closer they wheeled and closer still, till we could count the stripes of paint

on their faces and bodies and see each panting
pony's wide red nostrils " like pits full of blood to
the brim." We had been speaking in undertones
before, perhaps half-awed by the spectacle. Now
we all fell suddenly silent.

What did the Indians mean ? I cannot say
what was in other men's minds ; I only know
my own, and the thought that flashed up was
" Treachery ! " For the next instant there was
a terrific yell, and the whole line of Indians came
straight for us at the charge, firing their guns.
Yell followed yell, and the air was filled with crack-
ling rifle-shots and whizzing bullets. I saw Godfrey's
wife throw herself in front of him. Was it the
woman's sacrifice to shield her man from the leaden
hail, or to remind him to give her the merciful
bullet ?

" This is the end," I thought ; but the big General
in front stood like a rock.

Up, up they came, and then at the last second
their line split apart in the middle and each half
dashed by us to left and to right, the foam-flakes
from their snorting ponies floating to the ground
at our feet ; and then away in a cloud they dashed
off into the pines to reload their empty guns. We
stood unharmed.

The babel had stopped, and there was a great
silence. " Just a little game to try our nerves,"
said the General's firm voice to Captain Alexander.
" I knew they were only fooling with us when I
heard their bullets go high. But I want to compli-
ment that Mr. Shawano on his skill as a cavalry

leader. Won't you call him up for me, Mrs. God-frey ? " His eyes were still following the Indians, whom they had never left for a moment. Now for the first time he looked back.

But Mrs. Godfrey did not hear him ; her wonder-ful nerve had given way at last, and she lay in a dead faint in her husband's arms.

" She may be only a Ute half-breed," muttered Matthews, " but she's a white woman under her skin ! "

I did admire the splendid courage and coolness of the Governor in the face of that charge of 800 savage warriors. Had he shown a sign of flinching it is possible that some of us who were behind might have turned tail, and then who knows ? That wild charge might have become deadly earnest, and then every last one of us would have been wiped out.

But that very evening in the Ute camp I had a chance to see a courage and coolness displayed which I admired even more if possible. The Utes gave us a scalp-dance. They had always been enemies of the Plains Indians, and had lately gone down on the Plains for a buffalo hunt, and had returned triumphant ; they had got a splendid lot of robes, and, what was better than all, they had surprised some unlucky Cheyennes and had killed and scalped one of their braves and captured his little six-year-old son alive. The dance was a weird sight ; the firelight flickered on the naked painted bodies of the dancers and the fresh scalp hung waving in the wind on a pole in the centre

of the ring, and there, at the foot of the pole, alone in the midst of his enemies, danced the captive child. For hours I watched that baby ; he was helpless in the hands of his captors—he was put there to dance, and he danced ; but oh, how unwillingly. First one tiny foot was raised a bare half inch from the ground and then slowly set down again ; then the other was lifted the same way in its turn and as slowly set down—dance he must, and he knew it ; but it was the most lugubrious movement imaginable, and all the while I watched never once did that child look up, either to the scalp of his father waving over his head or to the ring of fierce faces, the faces of the deadly enemies of his tribe, that surrounded him.

" What will they do with him ? " I asked Godfrey, who also enjoyed the privilege of looking on at the spectacle.

" Can't say for certain," he answered. " The kid's obstinate as a pig now, but likely he'll forget his own people before long, and then the Utes will adopt him into their tribe and bring him up as a Ute. Maybe you'll see him on the war-path hunting for his Cheyenne uncle's scalp before he's twenty."

" But if he doesn't forget," I queried, " if he chooses to be a pig and remain obstinate, what then ? "

" Oh," said Godfrey, " in that case, likely they'll tie him to a stake and torture him next time they feel like having a circus. These Utes are bound to have a prisoner—it may be a Cheyenne or it may be another—every once in a while, to make a holy

show of. It relieves their feelings. But you and I won't get no tickets for that show. They'll take darned good care to keep it secret from the whites. Governor McCook here wouldn't stand no such performance."

To this day I cannot tell which I would put higher, the courage of the trained soldier, the man in charge, the Governor of the Territory, or that of the helpless Cheyenne boy alone in the midst of his enemies.

CHAPTER VII

WILD JUSTICE

RETURNING to Denver, I parted company with Matthews; to tell the truth, I was a bit tired of his everlasting sneers, so often (as I thought) directed against better men than himself. Besides, I thought I was competent now to stand on my own feet instead of going around on a personally conducted tour. Naturally my first step was to buy a horse. For this I went to Billy and Hi Ford, who had brought some 1500 head of wild bronco stock—bronco is Spanish for unbroken—from California to Denver where they were selling them as rapidly as they could get them broken in. Ford Brothers soon took my measure and for I think $60 fitted me out with a little brown mare, who had been ridden several times. They put me very carefully on her, and I went down the Platte a few miles and put up at a ranch. Along the main freighting roads most ranches would take you in overnight and give you supper, bed and breakfast for $1.50, or if your horse had to be fed also, for $2.25. A snowstorm came on that night and I lay there two days till the weather improved. The little brown mare had done herself uncommonly well in the barn, and

when I tried to climb on to her back on the third morning she began to play up. The friendly and much amused ranchman lent me a helping hand, however, and at last I got myself fixed in the saddle with my blanket-roll padding me in well there and the ranchman hanging tight on to her head.

" Do you think she'll buck ? " I asked nervously as he let her go.

" Guess so," said he.

And buck she certainly did. But I was so well wedged in with my pack that I did manage to remain, though I can't say I liked it, and the upshot of it was I rode her back to Denver and traded her (plus $20 more) to Billy Ford for an ancient chestnut " bronc " who had got over all his youthful frivolities. I called him Methusalem, and he turned out an excellent travelling animal for a tenderfoot. On him I rode out to Kiowa Creek to visit an English ranchman I had met in Denver, and I stayed there a few days riding around the prairie and seeing what cattle were like. My friend had a nice American wife and a nice bunch of American cattle, which he milked, while she, like a good ranchwoman, made butter from the milk. Butter was worth, I think, 75 cents a pound. Of course these American dairy cattle, which were just like our ordinary English farm stock, were quite unlike the long-horned, long-legged animals of Spanish breed, of which drovers had just begun to bring up large herds from Texas. The older Colorado stock-men, owners of American stock, rather resented this intrusion, as the wild Texas

brutes could be sold for less than half the prices they had been used to getting, and consequently their profits went down ; but they had to put up with it. All the disgruntled owner of American stock could do was to chase the others off his range when they invaded it, but this he had no legal right to do, as the range was Government land, and he only did it at the risk of rough handling from the Texas cowpunchers. Nevertheless, I did give my friend a hand at the game of driving them off in the absence of the cowpunchers, and I much enjoyed the good gallops on the prairie even though Methusalem was hardly fast enough to head a wild steer. But I did get my first taste of cowpunching and liked it well.

Next I decided to wander down the Platte and see what that section was like. Ranches extended some fifty odd miles below Denver, about to the point where the South Platte River makes its big bend eastwards, and at this point a new town was just being started. It was named Evans in honour of the man who had been Governor of Colorado before McCook, and its *raison d'être* was that the first railroad into Colorado was now being opened so far for traffic. This railroad was the Denver Pacific R.R. running from Cheyenne to Denver, and Evans was the half-way house. The city was just three weeks old when I got there, and the site of it was on the north bank of the Platte, across which a bridge was going to be built. I put up at the ranch of a very friendly old ranchman, Godfrey, no relation to the other Godfrey down at Saguache ;

he had a bunch of American cattle, and a wife and son, the latter a very fine young fellow.   Godfrey let me use his rifle, an old-fashioned small-bored muzzle-loader with a heavy octagon barrel nearly four feet long, I should say.   Armed with this wondrous weapon I sallied out after antelopes, of which there were any number around there, and I got my first lessons in stalking.   Stalking antelope, like everything else, was quite new to me, and I was as keen as possible to take lessons in whatever thing there was to be learnt.   There was something, though, to be learnt in that little mushroom city of Evans which I most certainly did not anticipate.   When I rode over there I found that it consisted of some forty or fifty houses of raw boards, mostly half-finished or with their roofs in process of being " shingled," stuck down here and there on the bare prairie.   The parched yellow bunch-grass, over which wild Texas cattle had grazed a month before, grew up to, and under, the little frame buildings which were raised for the most part six inches or a foot off the ground on stone or brick props ;   the earth was cut up in every direction by the ruts of waggon-wheels, and piles of newly sawn lumber lay about.   In the middle of all snorted the locomotive, the earliest that ever ran on the plains of Colorado—for the railroad had come at last, and this was the end of the track, the first completed section of the iron road, in Colorado Territory.

I was riding past a bar-room where were some men with whisky bottles and glasses set out before them, when one of them sung out to me :

"Come 'n hev' a drink."

"No, thank you," I replied without pulling up.

In a moment out flashed a revolver pointed straight at my head.

"Yes, you will," said the same voice with emphasis, "or else——"

What "else" meant was left to the imagination, but I didn't find it hard to guess. My reply was:

"Oh, certainly," and I sprang from my saddle saying, "I'd rather drink than be shot any day." And without more ado I took my dose. But I can't say I liked my society.

"I've looked to see 'em have a man for breakfast any morning," said old Godfrey when I got back to the ranch and told him of it. "According to what I hear they've bin shooting at the lamps in the saloons and dancing on the bars, slinging their six-shooters round their heads, and raising Cain generally, every night. I've wondered there hasn't been nobody shot yet, but I reckon they were each one of 'em kind of shy of being the first to begin. But now, if they've started in, likely they'll have another Julesburg here if they ain't interfered with."

Julesburg, as I have already said, was a spot that had been the end of the track on the Union Pacific Railroad for some months during its construction, and it had been, perhaps, the most debauched and the most blood-stained little moral pesthouse the Far West ever saw. A young man presently arrived at Godfrey's where he also found quarters under that hospitable roof; he called

himself a schoolmaster by trade, and his object was to see if by chance such a thing was wanted in this three-weeks'-old town. A town, even the newest, almost always had some families, and that generally meant some boys of school age, with, as the obvious and natural consequence, an opening for a schoolmaster. I can't say that I was much impressed with my new friend's scholastic qualifications, but I was out to learn all I could of this strange country, and at his invitation I rode with him down to the ford across the South Platte with a view to seeing what opening there might be in Evans. " Crack " came the sharp sound of a pistol-shot as we rode through the icy ford, and we saw men running among the houses, and a couple of horsemen with rifles in their hands galloping after a man who was flying at top speed towards the brush in the Platte bottom.

" The toughs from Cheyenne have been trying to run this town ever since it was started," said my companion, " but they haven't killed anyone so far. I wonder if that shot means the first man killed."

We rode through the fringe of willow brush and cotton-wood trees that skirted the river, and up the bluff. We had now got fairly into the town and saw all the population—all the male population, that is—swarming like bees in the middle of the main street. Horses and ox-teams stood here and there untended ; the shingling hatchets and carpenter's tools lay around the half-finished houses, just where they had been thrown down. The stores were open, but they were empty, for buyers

and sellers had crowded, like all the rest, to the scene of action. There in the centre of the crowd was a sight to remember. Ten men shoulder to shoulder formed a ring, each man facing outwards, each man holding his cocked revolver, muzzle up, the hand that held it being on a level with his chest ; the men's set mouths and searching eyes, turning restlessly on the crowd around, showed them to be sharply on the watch for signs of an attempted rescue.

A rescue, but of whom ? It did not take long to recognize who was the object of their care. In the middle of the ring, bareheaded, with his arms bound, stood a prisoner, a sickly smile on his loose lips, and the colour coming and going in patches on his bloated face. By him was a guard, also pistol in hand like those who formed the ring, but his eyes were bent not on the crowd, but on the prisoner ; and the pistol he held was pointed not towards the sky, but straight at the prisoner's heart. Were a rescue attempted, it was clear the rescuers would recover only a corpse. That the toughs would try to set their friend free if they dared was certain ; it was useless to try to secure him by locking him up in an extempore gaol, for there was no building in the town that could resist a determined assault for five minutes ; but a bodyguard such as now held him could not be maintained for long. These men had their own business to attend to ; and standing guard, pistol in hand, expecting to kill or be killed, is a dead loss of time and wages. However, it was not intended by those

who were putting their energies, heart and soul, into the building of a new town to waste very much time over guarding a murderer. For it was murder that this wretched captive was held for, and stiff and stark, in a house hard by, with a bullet through his brain, lay the body of his victim. The sound of the loud weeping of the widowed wife and orphan daughters was heard at intervals across the vacant lots, and that agonized crying served to inflame the passions of the crowd. From the bystanders I gathered that old man Steel, a most respectable man who kept a boarding-house, had just been shot by a tough, and that it was more than probable that Judge Lynch would take cognizance of the case. The crying of the wretched widow and orphaned children sounded in the ears of the people, and called for vengeance. The one anxiety was, would the other railroad toughs try to rescue their hero?

Presently an empty lumber waggon was run out a little way from the town on the bare prairie ; from the box end of this a few nail kegs were arranged in a double row, perhaps eight feet apart, and boards were laid on them for seats. A man sprang up on the waggon, and said:

" A crime has been committed here, and I move that a People's Court be constituted to try the case. Those in favour will say ' Aye.' "

" Aye, aye," came from all quarters, like a dropping fire.

" Contrary, ' No,' " the temporary chairman added, as if by an afterthought.

I fancied I heard a few muttered remarks, but no man said "No" openly. Perhaps the railroad toughs were lying low for the present.

Up jumped another man, so quick and pat that it dawned upon me that there was a prepared scheme being put in operation.

"I move that Captain Sopris be elected judge of this court," he said.

As before, the "Ayes" had it.

"Captain Sopris was a People's Judge in Denver, and he hanged a heap of men there, too, time of the Pike's Peak boom," said an old-timer near me. "The captain knows the ropes." There was a grim double meaning in the way he said "ropes."

Captain Sopris mounted the waggon box in his turn and took his seat, throwing a keen eye over the crowd.

"Gentlemen," he said, "I have been elected to try this case by you, the people. Is it your will that I should select a jury? Those who are in favour say 'Aye!'"

Once more the full-throated chorus of "Ayes!" arose from the crowd.

"Contrary, 'No,'" said the judge to the crowd in matter-of-fact tones, turning at the same time to speak to a man beside him. It was his art, I think, to appear to take it all as mere matter of course, yet I am certain he and his supporters were sharply on the watch for any sign of opposition from the prisoner's friends. But the "people" had got a leader now, and any who would have liked to interfere were cowed by the almost unani-

mous ' Aye ! ' " of the majority. When the judge said " Contrary, ' No ! ' " there may have been a murmur here and there, but no man durst answer " No," square and bold.

The people were rousing to their work. We were all packed tight round the court, for that farm waggon and the nail keg seats had become the Court of the People out there on the prairie under the open sky. I had dismounted and wedged myself in next the seats where my neighbour said the jury would be. Quickly a dozen jurors were chosen and took their places. A Bible was produced, and every juror was sworn to give an honest verdict. Each man as soon as he was sworn took his seat, on one or other of the impromptu benches, till there were six on one side and six on the other.

" And now," said the judge, " bring in the prisoner."

Accordingly the guards, with the prisoner in their midst, moved up to the open side of the court ; but as they did so it was seen that something had occurred, for beside the prisoner stood little Pat Egan, who was believed to represent the majesty of the law in some sort of capacity or other.

" Captain Sopris," he began in somewhat plaintive accents, " this hyar thing ain't reg'lar at all. By rights this hyar man's my prisoner, and I can't consent to no proceedings of this sort."

The judge took no more notice of him than if he had been a piece of wood ; less, indeed, for he did not appear to see him.

" But," continued the little Irishman, " I'm a

county officer, I am, and I'm liable to be called in question for this business. And I can't give up this man," he went on piteously, " without some excuse, ye know I can't."

The audience smiled audibly, but the judge, the jury and guards never looked at him, never heard him, never knew he was there, so to speak, but went on with their own business, arranging the order in which the witnesses should be called.

Pat Egan continued his pitiful demands for an excuse. The crowd was jammed thick round the court, the foremost men leaning over the backs of the jury on both sides. Eager to catch every word, I had tied my horse to a post in the street and had squeezed myself in up to the very seat where the jury sat, so that I was within a couple of yards of Mr. Egan and the prisoner. Leaning on me was a great yellow-bearded giant in a slouch hat. He reached down to his hip and produced an enormous revolver, one of the old dragoon Colt's, with a barrel about a foot long. Bearing on my shoulder with his left hand, he extended his long right arm over the heads of the jury till the pistol-muzzle was within a few inches of Pat's head. Pat, with his face to the judge's bench, was still volubly explaining that he was a county officer and couldn't consent.

" Mr. Egan," breathed the giant with the big pistol, in the softest tones.

Mr. Egan was absorbed in his own ardent utterances, and didn't hear.

" Mr. Egan," a little louder.

Pat turned round sharp and looked into the muzzle of the formidable weapon.

" Mr. Egan, will that do ye for an excuse ? " said the giant with an air of gentle sarcasm.

Mr. Egan recoiled several feet with an air of comic alarm.

" Oh, certainly, sir," he responded with alacrity. " Certainly, certainly, quite sufficient ; that will do." And he, the sole representative of the lawful Government of Colorado, disappeared promptly and finally from the scene.

And now the serious business of the court began.

" Is there a lawyer in town ? " asked the judge. " If so, fetch him. The prisoner can have counsel."

There was a Mr. Tallboys, a lawyer, a very young one, who came. The people of this mushroom town had arrived with a rush from everywhere, and every profession was represented.

" Understand," said Sopris, leaning over from the waggon to the counsel for the accused, " this is a People's Court. Any arguments you can use for your client will get a fair hearing. But you are not to object to the competence of the court. If you try to do so, I am deaf."

The lawyer, looking very uncomfortable, murmured some indistinct answer. He was in an extremely irregular and unpleasant position. But he saw that he must either accept it or go. He elected to stay. As counsel for the prisoner, he stood beside him in the centre of the court.

" I shall now call on the prosecution to bring forward their witnesses," said Captain Sopris. " We

will hear their story first, and you, prisoner, can cross-examine them either by yourself or by your lawyer."

The first witness came forward and, after having been sworn on the Book to tell the truth, the whole truth, and nothing but the truth, began :

"I was at dinner at old man Steel's boarding-house. It was the first table and it was chock-full. This man come in—he was a boarder there too—and wanted to find a place, and growled because he couldn't get none. Then one of Mr. Steel's gals who was waiting at table told him he must wait till his turn, till there was room. Wal', he says something sassy to her, and she up and slaps a cup of coffee she had in her hand right in his face. Then he begun to get up on his ear about it, and so two or three of the young fellows at table jest fired him out."

The judge, who was sitting reflectively on the waggon-box, with his head on his hand, here interposed.

"Did they hit him or pound him at all ? "

"No," answered the witness, "not nohow. They jest took him by the shoulders and jest naturally fired him out'n the door. He'd had a drink or two in him, you know, though he warn't drunk."

"What did he do then ? " asked one of the jury.

"Went off, I reckon," said the witness. "I didn't see no more of him."

"Did Mr. Steel have anything to do with turning him out ? " asked the judge.

" No, sir. He warn't thar' ; he was in the inner room, I reckon."

" Did you see the shooting ? " asked the judge.

" No, sir, I went off to my work as soon as dinner was over," was the reply.

" Mr. Tallboys, do you wish to ask this witness any questions ? " said the judge to the prisoner's lawyer.

The lawyer conferred a minute with his client, and then said to the court that he didn't wish to cross-examine this man. The witness, a young carpenter, was accordingly told he could go, which he did with an air of very considerable relief, mingling at once with the crowd. Another man was now brought forward and sworn like the first.

" Were you with Mr. Steel after dinner ? " asked the judge.

" Yes," said the witness, " I was."

" Tell the jury what happened."

" Mr. Steel and I were unloading a load of lumber I'd brought for him ; he was at one end of the pile, I was at the other, and we were lifting the boards off the waggon. Suddenly I saw the prisoner come up behind Mr. Steel, and I heard him say ' I want to talk to you.' "

" Was the prisoner alone ? " asked a juryman.

" I didn't see anyone, not to say actually with him. There were two or three men standing together across the street, but I don't know for certain as they had anything to do with him."

" What did Mr. Steel say ? " asked the judge.

" He looks at him, and says he, ' I can't talk to

you now : I'm busy. You must come around
after working hours.' Then the prisoner says,
' You've got to talk to me, and you've got to talk
to me now.' And Mr. Steel he says, ' Wal', I ain't
agoin' to,' and turned round to take hold of the
lumber again ; and the prisoner, he reaches down
and pulls out his pistol, and, before I could holler
to him or do anything, he just put it close behind
Mr. Steel's head and fired. Mr. Steel dropped, and
the prisoner he ran. I started round the waggon
to grab him, but he ran t'other way. Then I picked
up Mr. Steel ; he was breathing, but he never spoke.
The bullet went in at the back of his head, and
come out over his right eye. Me and some more
took him into the house."

" Mr. Tallboys, have you any question to ask
this witness ? " said Captain Sopris.

Mr. Tallboys consulted with the prisoner awhile,
and announced that he had not. The witness, a
teamster, was accordingly dismissed, like the former
one. Three or four more were called, and repeated
the story told by these two in much the same words.
It was elicited that the prisoner had had no pistol
on when he came to dinner and was put out of
doors, so that he must have procured it in the
interval before he came back. The case was so
clear that there was no necessity to distress those
poor unhappy women by calling them.

One of the men who captured the prisoner testified
that he was at work near, and " Happened to have
a saddled horse near, and a Winchester handy."
Also that he had a friend similarly provided.

Tenderfoot though I was, it dawned on me that these men must belong to an organized body who had made themselves ready beforehand. Evans had its Vigilantes. The two friends heard a shot, saw a man with a pistol running for the brush, heard the people crying murder, and at once set after him. He just got to cover as they caught him up, but he showed no fight ; as soon as they covered him with the Winchesters he threw up his hands and surrendered, and here he was.

Here the lawyer saw his chance to put a few questions in cross-examination, asking whether they promised the prisoner his life when he surrendered, and so forth ; but nothing came out that could help him. Things looked terribly black for the wretched man, and he began to cry.

Nothing could have been more orderly than the behaviour of the court. While the witnesses were being examined you might have heard a pin drop. Between whiles the crowd conversed among themselves, but in sober and hushed tones. There was no yelling of a mob for the blood of a victim, but a most evident deadly resolution to exact the uttermost penalty. I remember thinking to myself, " How I wish Carlyle were here " (he was still alive in those days), " to feel for himself the contrast between this and the revolutionary tribunals of Paris ! This would seem to him more like some old Teuton gathering of freemen in the Northern forests."

And now the witnesses were all disposed of, and the trial drew to its close. The young lawyer

was asked if he had any witnesses to call for the defence, but he intimated that there were none. I felt for the young man in his first case, with such a hopeless task before him as the defence of this red-handed criminal taken in the very act. I racked my brain to think of what I should say were I in his position. I thought of the words of Magna Charta (remember I had only just left Cambridge):
" Against no man will we go, neither will we send, save by lawful judgment of his peers, and by the law of the land."

" The common law holds good in America," I thought, " and surely they will have heard of Magna Charta." Then I heard the judge's grave tones addressing the lawyer.

" Mr. Tallboys," he said, " the evidence in this case is now before the court ; but before the jury retire to consider their verdict you are at liberty to offer any remarks you have to make on it that you may think advisable. Understand, you are not to question in any way the competency of the court. This is a people's court, sprung from and organized by the people themselves, and if you question its right you put yourself out of court at once, and it will be my duty not to hear you. On the question of the prisoner's guilt you are at full liberty to speak."

These words scattered to the winds my imaginary reference to Magna Charta and the field of Runnimede and the long tradition of Anglo-Norman law. They were all ruled out of court. The issue was narrowed down to the simple question, " Did

the prisoner kill old man Steel or no ? " and to that, after the testimony of several witnesses to a thing that had happened two hours before in broad daylight under the open sky, but one answer was possible.

The lawyer got up and spoke a few words, but there really was nothing for him to say.

" Gentlemen of the jury," said Captain Sopris, " I think the case is complete, but before you retire to consider your verdict I will ask the prisoner personally to make any statement he thinks fit that might weigh with you. Prisoner, have you anything to say ? "

There was a great silence of the whole crowd for some minutes ; all eyes were bent on the man addressed. He swallowed hard a few times, and choked back his tears, and at last whined out :

" I didn't mean to hurt him."

Didn't mean to hurt him—when he had shot him through the head at two yards off ! If it had not been a tragedy there would have been a shout of laughter. But, instead, there was a grimmer silence than before. The prisoner had said all he had to say.

The pause was broken by Captain Sopris.

" Gentlemen of the jury, you have heard the evidence, and also what the prisoner has to say for himself. You will now retire to consider your verdict."

The jury rose and filed out, and standing off a little distance on the prairie talked together. The tension in the court was relaxed, and there was

a hum of conversation. The prisoner whispered to his lawyer inaudibly.

Presently the jury filed back into court and sat down.

" Gentlemen," said Captain Sopris, " have you decided on your verdict ? "

" We have," answered one who acted as foreman.

" Are you unanimous ? " again asked the judge.

" We are," was again the answer.

" What is your verdict ? "

There was a breathless hush in the court as the foreman said in clear steady tones :

" Guilty of murder in the first degree."

Again you might have heard a pin drop on the prairie grass.

I saw the two men with the Winchesters slip on to their saddle-horses and take up their position on the side between the crowd on the prairie and the town.

Sopris raised his eyes from the jury to the crowd.

" Gentlemen," he said, " the jury have found the prisoner guilty of murder in the first degree. It is for you, the people, to say what his punishment shall be. Those who are in favour of hanging will say ' Aye.' "

An answering roar of " Aye " went up to the sky above us.

" Contrary, ' No,' " said Sopris.

There was a dead silence.

Sopris waited to give any friend of the prisoner time to harden his heart and say " No." None did.

" Prisoner," said the judge, turning to the

wretched creature, who was now sobbing and unnerved, "the jury have found you guilty and the people have sentenced you to be hung. You will be hung in fifteen minutes to the nearest tree. If you have anything to say before then, you had better say it."

Then was heard a loud voice from the outskirts of the crowd. It came from a big man, sitting on a horse, with a sixteen-shot Winchester in his hand ; two more horsemen, similarly armed, were by him.

"Every man come down to the tree," he said. "Let no man stay back. It's one and all."

"One and all." It was the motto, if I remember right, of the New Model Army in its struggle with the Rump, that terrible Cromwellian army that did not shrink from cutting off the head of a king. And indeed I asked myself how far was the court, presided over by Mr. President Bradshaw, which sentenced Charles I, more legal than this people's court, with Captain Sopris as elected judge ? "These Americans," thought I, "are the real true-bred sons of those old Commonwealth men."

Slowly across the trampled grass the procession moved towards the fatal tree. The sun was sinking fast towards the west, where the great jagged wall of the Rocky Mountains stood dark against the clear sky. Just outside the town, on the edge of the bottom lands of the Platte, grew a big cotton-wood tree, its leafless branches spreading wide. Here we halted. I had remounted my pony and, anxious to see the whole thing through, had wedged

myself into the middle of the throng. One of the
guards stepped up to me, and, holding up his pistol
as he laid his hand on my bridle, said :

" Get off that horse."

" What for ? " I asked. " Why do you want
him ? "

" Never mind," was his answer, " you shall
have him back again ; but he's wanted. You've
got to get off."

His manner was peremptory. I dismounted.
They took my picket rope, a nearly new one, three-
quarters of an inch in diameter and forty feet long,
and, making a noose in one end, tossed it over a
limb twelve or fifteen feet up from the ground.

" Will you tell us," said the leader of the Vigilantes, addressing the condemned man, " who gave
you the pistol ? "

I gathered from his manner that he had been
trying to induce him to reveal his accomplices
on the way to the tree. The wretch looked up
at the rope swinging above him, and said :

" Will you give me my life if I tell ? "

" We promise nothing," said his questioner,
a short bullet-headed man with a singularly resolute
face, " but," he added, " it won't be worse for
you if you do."

" Then I won't say," answered the prisoner.

" Have you any friends that you want to say
good-bye to ? " he asked again ; and, the prisoner
nodding assent, he called out to the crowd, " If
there are any friends of this man here who wish to
speak to him, they can do so, one at a time."

A dissolute-looking gambler in a very seedy frock-coat, with his hands in his pockets, slouched forward with an uneasy swagger. The guards examined him to see that he had no concealed weapons, and then admitted him to the prisoner. He sauntered up to him with an ill-concealed nervousness which he tried to carry off as easy nonchalance.

" Wal', Joe, old man," he observed to his friend, " you've got to the jumping-off place this time, I guess."

The prisoner gave a ghastly grin.

" Say, old man," he continued, drawing one hand from his trousers' pocket, and rubbing it on the unshaven cheek of the condemned man, where three or four days' stubbly growth of hair bristled, " you'd better ax 'em to let you shave this off. It might be in the way of the rope."

The prisoner only groaned at the disgusting pleasantry.

" Take him away," said the leader to the guards. " No more of this. Now," he said to the doomed man, " do you want to pray ? Will you have a minister ? "

No answer was returned ; but there was a slight movement among the crowd—men looking to right and left as if searching for the sight of a black coat ; but it was in vain—no one like a minister was to be found.

" Do you wish to send a message to anybody ? " asked the leader.

" I've a wife in Philadelphia," said the murderer through his sobs.

A notebook was instantly produced.

" Your name, your real name ? " said the Vigilante.

" Joe Carr."

" Her address ? "

The prisoner mumbled something I couldn't hear. It was a hangman's knot that had been tied in my rope, and now the noose was put over his head, and settled round his neck ; the other end of the rope tossed over the bough was made fast with a turn round the trunk of the tree ; the horse was brought alongside him.

" Now say a prayer if you want to," said the Vigilante.

" I'll be good God damned if I think a prayer of mine 'ud go more'n seven feet high," said the reprobate.

In a moment he was hoisted on to the horse, the rope drawn taut, and a resounding smack given to the horse's quarters. The animal bounded forward, and the murderer was left swinging.

" Run him up ! run him up ! " was the cry, and twenty willing hands hauled on the rope till the body was swung aloft to within two feet of the bough, and the rope was again made fast.

There was silence for a little space ; then the leader of the Vigilantes took his stand beneath the fatal branch, and spoke short and plain.

" There's men here," said he, " as guilty in intention as that man," pointing to the body, " was in act. Let this be a warning to them. Let this be a sign that in this town the people don't mean to tolerate any such goings on. We know there

were men who encouraged this miserable wretch
to do this thing that brought him to this—yes,
and lent him the pistol to do it with. They may
thank their stars they are not hanging beside him
now. They are just as guilty as he was, and if
they know what's healthy for them they'll get out
of this before daylight to-morrow. And I say the
same to any more there are of the same kidney
here, and who thought they were going to run this
town. They'd better drop it. They'd better get.
The people of this town are going to run this town
themselves, and this here is the proof of it. Enough
said." And, turning away, he stepped back into
the crowd and joined his friends.

"It's all over, boys," said the big man on the
horse, with the Winchester in his hand. "We
can go back to our business now. Let no man
interfere with that body," he added. "It'll be
seen to to-night. No one's to touch it without
orders."

And the crowd broke up into knots and slowly
dispersed.

"Young man," said one of the guards to me,
leading up my pony, "here's your bronco. You
shall have your rope back in the morning; it's
occupied at present. No one will trouble you
over this matter; it was taken from you by force,
you understand."

And then I understood that the demonstration
of holding up a pistol when I was told to dismount
had been really for my benefit, to relieve me of
responsibility, if by any chance the proper officers

of the ordinary law of the territory should take any notice of this day's work.

I took my horse, mounted him, and later on, when the crowd had dispersed, rode down to the ford. The pony stopped in mid-channel to drink, and I shall not forget the scene. The sun was just setting behind the range of the Rocky Mountains, and in the foreground stood the withered cotton-wood with its ghastly fruit. The work was done.

So far as I know, the regular law took no notice. The effects of the action of the Vigilantes were, however, marked and immediate. That night many of the worst characters in town left it, some in their haste walking all the way to Denver to get clear of a spot so ominous to them. The rowdyism, the displaying of revolvers and shooting at lamps out of bravado, stopped instanter. There never was another man shot in the town of Evans for two years, and then the shooting was accidental, though, as the man who fired the rifle on that occasion happened to have had words with the man who was wounded—it was not a fatal shot—he was most terribly frightened, fully expecting the Vigil-antes to get after him.

This rapid and most surprising purification of the moral atmosphere of Evans City did, I admit, dispose me at the time to think favourably of the action of lynch law. But five years' residence in the territory was enough to alter my opinion. During that time only one man was legally executed there, and he was a foreigner and a poor man ; and, moreover, there is reason to believe that his crime

only amounted to manslaughter. Yet during those years many crimes of violence were committed, and many lynchings occurred. Some of these were, I make no doubt, as well deserved as the one of which I was a witness ; others very probably were not—for instance, two men, if not three, were lynched, on one of the creeks that run from the Divide, for killing a calf. But the general effect of the system upon the administration of the ordinary law was simply disastrous. Whenever atrocious murderers are hanged as soon as caught, there arises at once a strong presumption that a man-slayer, who is left to be dealt with by an ordinary jury, has probably much to excuse him. This feeling vastly increased the difficulty of getting juries to convict. Popular criminals are quite sure to get off, and the ordinary law becomes glaringly ineffective and sinks into something very like contempt, while the lynchers alone are really dreaded. And this very dread increases crime, because horse-thieves and cattle-thieves, when pursued, know they will probably be lynched, and never hesitate to shoot, thinking they may as well be hanged for killing a man as for killing a calf. Every thief becomes a potential murderer, and goes armed. Peaceful citizens arm themselves in defence of their lives and property, and, as collisions will occur, crimes of violence naturally abound. The remedy is worse than the disease.

CHAPTER VIII

OUR LOST PARADISE

I RETURNED from Evans to Denver feeling more strongly than ever the attraction of the cattle business in this glorious country of unlimited free range, but I had not quite made up my mind as yet to go in for it. Also, before deciding, there was still one place I particularly wanted to see, the Wet Mountain Valley, of which I had heard men speak very highly. I was told that the whole floor of the valley was open grazing land like the Plains, but it was shut in by pine-clad mountains, which provided splendid natural shelter for stock. So I struck out for Cañon City on Methusalem, knowing that from there some sort of road or trail into the Valley could be found. Stopping overnight at a ranch on Fountain Creek on my road, a man told me that, if I cared to ride off my route for a mile or so up the cañon where the creek came out of the mountains, I should there behold the sight of my life.

" That's a real big spring of pure soda-water," he explained, " bubbling up into a great basin out of the solid rock, and from thar' it runs over and tumbles into the Fountain Creek ; you never saw the like of it in all your born days."

So as I was not in any special hurry, I did ride up there and found it just as he had said. What I saw was a beautiful wild cañon, with scrub oak growing along the creek and glorious pines standing up on the rocky mountain walls that shut it in ; and here was actually the great soda spring, in a basin of its own, some ten feet across, and it did bubble over and run down into the creek below. I was not geologist enough to say what the rocks were, or why this extraordinary mineral spring should have its birth there, but I could feel at least that I was face to face with a most striking marvel of Nature. The spot was wonderfully wild. An old Indian trail ran up the cañon, and there were the blackened circles of some camp fires, indeed I am not sure that there was not a square of logs put together as a camp site, but no other sign of man's presence was visible save one : on a bush hard by, I saw, hanging, a number of little bits of coloured rags and odds and ends of buckskin. This made me think of how I had seen, beside holy wells in the south of Ireland, bushes similarly hung with little bits of rag. In Ireland, of course, these were the mementoes of Roman Catholic pilgrims, left behind them in token of their visit to a sacred spot, very often in gratitude for a cure attributed to the power of the saint to whom the well was sacred. " But," said I to myself, " there aren't many Roman Catholic pilgrims out here in Colorado, and I shouldn't suppose that they'd started any holy wells yet." It never dawned on me that the Indians also

regarded certain springs as holy, and had got the same idea of leaving mementoes of their visits in honour of the spirits they imagined to be the guardians of the sacred spot. Yet so it was, and shortly after, when I got to Cañon City, a man there who knew about the Indians explained to me their attitude of mind with regard to spirits and natural marvels.

The cañon where the soda spring burst out was quite narrow, and no sort of place for a ranch; the idea of myself or anyone else ever wanting to settle there never dawned upon my simple mind. It does fairly make me smile now to think of it. Anybody who liked might have taken up that spring then with 160 acres of land, either free as a homestead, or as a pre-emption for $1.25 an acre. Men had known of it for ten years past and none had cared to do this. You couldn't buy that spring now, or rather the six springs— for I believe there are six of them, all different— not for a million of dollars. The place became the famous Manitou Springs, Manitou being the Indian name for the Great Spirit to whom it was sacred, and the white men very sensibly adopting the Indian title for it. The place is now celebrated all over the world for its cures. And thus I missed becoming a millionaire; but that is the way in which one misses one's chances in this life. So I left the wonderful spring to take care of itself and made my way on to Cañon City.

There not only did I hear about the Indian attitude towards the supernatural, but I got another

piece of information, one which rather put me off Wet Mountain Valley. A Prussian officer was said to have arranged to plant 300 German settlers in the Valley. His scheme was to plough up the rich bottom lands along the creeks which carried plenty of water to irrigate with, while the settlers' cattle could roam at will over the free pasture in the rest of the Valley. This was enough to discourage any dreams I might have of starting a cattle ranch there; still, as I already had come so far to see the place, I decided to go in. I had rather a cold trip of it, for it was now December, and the mercury sometimes went down to zero, aye, and below zero, though so far there was little snow. But every creek formed ice along its banks, and winter was fairly on us. There were only as yet four settlers in the whole Valley when I reached it, and certainly the beauty of the Valley had not been exaggerated to me: I did not wonder that the poor Utes had kicked about giving it up. It was full of game, and there were still some herds of antelope running there, for the hunters and ranchmen had not yet killed them out; while the forests round were full of deer. The huge range of the Sangre de Cristo Mountains, near 14,000 feet high, shut off the Valley on the west side from the San Luis Park. I spent quite a long time down there with an old hunter and trapper named Horn, who had a cabin on one of the side gulches, and I visited his traps with him and listened to the wonderful yarns he told of his many years of adventurous life out on the Ragged Edge.

But for myself, thinking things all over, I came to the conclusion that the Wet Mountain Valley, beautiful as it was, did not offer the best prospects for a ranch, and somewhat regretfully at last I came away from it.

Extracts from old letters and diaries are apt to pall in a book of reminiscences, and I do not intend often to fall back upon that refuge of the destitute, but I think I will just put in here one extract from one of my letters to my mother, which may help to give an idea of how things struck me at the time :

" . . . My Christmas was spent in the cabin of old Horn, the hunter, and on Christmas Day the cabin got on fire, and we spent most of the day in putting it out with a bucket and two tin cups. However, our primitive fire-engine was successful. The valley is very beautiful, fertile, and well watered. I do not know whether it is marked in the map, but it is the valley immediately north-west of the head of the Huerfano (pronounced Wharfăno). Coming back I took rather a different route ; for, by the way I came, I had to ford the Arkansas. This was not pleasant, as the stream was running strong and large pieces of loose ice came rushing down. It was long before I could get my pony to face it, for the moment he got in and the ice struck him he plunged back again, but at last by a vigorous use of the spur I got him through all right. To avoid this ford, however, I followed an Indian trail down through

the mountains on the south bank. I had to walk all the way, as the hills were very steep and the trail narrow. In one place we had to cross a small river which had been flooded and frozen over, but the ice in the middle had broken away so that it could neither be jumped nor forded. At last, I found a narrow bridge of ice right across. So I got sand and sanded it all the way over, and then with some trouble brought the pony over. It was barely a foot wide in the middle, and he did not like it, but there was no other way, as the cañon above and below was impassable. As we emerged from the hills I found I had dropped a blanket, so I went back for it and on the way I saw two large deer. I hunted them some time but could not get a shot. The buck had the finest horns I have seen. You need not alarm yourself about my solitary journeys, for there are no hostile Indians here, and I always go well armed. I think of returning to the Eastern States for a bit in the spring, but do not know when or where. . . ."

The plan indicated in my letter was carried out. I did take a trip back to New York and Boston later in the spring to visit kind friends I had in both those cities, but I had already pretty well made up my mind to become a ranchman, and a month or so of the civilized East did not shake me in that determination. So in the early summer I quitted Boston and once more took the cars for the Wild West, and having got there proceeded likewise to take a partner and arrange

to take up a ranch. My partner was Lew Howell, a man whom I had got to know in Denver, and I believe I met him first at Gus Cheever's office there, where I was at once greatly attracted by him. To give some idea of the impression Lew could make upon a stranger at first sight, I will here quote the account given of him by a witness who really has got him down to a hair. My witness is Miss Kingsley, daughter of Charles Kingsley, whom I well remembered as a professor at Cambridge, and a sister of Maurice Kingsley, who was up at Trinity with me and subsequently became secretary to the company that founded Colorado Springs. It was there at the Springs, two or three years after this date, that she saw Lew Howell, and here is what she says :

" Yesterday afternoon, as M. and I were sitting in the office, the door opened, and in walked a man followed by a large saffron-coloured bulldog, called Rattler. This man, whom M. knew very well, is the most thorough specimen of a Western man I have yet seen to speak to. He was dressed in apparently five or six flannel shirts, two undercoats, thick trousers tucked into long boots, a light-blue soldier's great-coat with capes, under which knife, pistol and powder-flask peeped out, and a slouched felt hat completed the costume. As I sat listening to his yarns to M., I could have fancied myself reading a chapter of Catlin. Here was the real thing. A finely made young fellow about twenty-eight, with bright blue eyes and brown

hair and beard, up to anything, from shooting a wolf to riding 240 miles in thirty-six hours to catch a prisoner; yet civil and courteous to me in the extreme. All the time he was here I never heard a single bad word from him, though I saw that he caught himself up short two or three times. It was strange, seeing and hearing with one's own eyes and ears, what one has read of since childhood." [1]

Well, all I can say is that her description fits Lew to the life and is done a great deal more brilliantly than I could hope to do it. Lew Howell certainly had a very taking way with him, and that was undoubtedly why I took him as a partner. I think Gus Cheever somewhat doubted the wisdom of this step, but he may also have reflected that such a tenderfoot as I still was might so very easily do very much worse. To be sure, Lew had no capital, and though he and I were proposing to start a ranch together, he was no more a ranchman than I was myself; but he did have a wide experience on the frontier and he bore a good character. He was at this time an employé in the U.S. Mint at Denver, where his particular job was to run the steam-engine. He was unmarried, and what he did with his pay was to support his mother and an invalid sister. His father was a Virginian, who had some money; he brought out a waggon-train across the Plains, and set up a stamp-mill for crushing ore up in the mines. Unfortunately, the ores didn't pay, and the mill

[1] *South by West.* By Miss Kingsley.

was a failure. Mr. Howell had been a religious man back in Wisconsin, where they had lived before coming out to Colorado ; he had been a deacon there, or something high-toned like that. Unfortunately, as Lew put it, his religion didn't pay freight across the Plains when freights were 25 cents per lb., and Mr. Howell ended by deserting his family and his wife and going off with another woman. Lew, much to his credit, had supported the family by his labour ever since. The unhappy sister was an epileptic, who was subject to the most awful fits at intervals, in which she was capable of saying or doing dreadful things. When she was sane she was pleasant enough ; the mother, who was immensely stout and had a rather violent temper, devoted herself to the unhappy daughter and nursed her in her attacks with assiduous solicitude. I am bound to say that there was no attempt made to conceal from me the internal difficulties of the household ; I was not roped in and I went into the thing with my eyes open. The other member of the family was an eighteen-year-old son who bore the curious name of Doctor Adoniram Judson Howell. His father during his religious period back there in the States before his religion declined to pay freight across the Plains had named his youngest son after a certain distinguished missionary to Burmah, whom he admired. Jud Howell was a tall, vigorous youth, and was at this time working, if I remember rightly, in a Denver lumber-yard.

Lew and I were puzzled as to where to take up a ranch. He rather favoured the Plains where

there were 500 miles of open pasture towards the east. The drawback was the hostility of the Plains Indians, Sioux, Arapahoes, Cheyennes and Kiowas. But ex-Governor A. C. Hunt, a great friend of Lew's, liked the Plains, and his judgment inclined Lew in that direction. But I could only say that I didn't know the Plains except from the windows of the railroad cars, and I thought they were rather exposed. What struck my fancy was the San Luis Park, so praised by Governor Gilpin, and especially the Saguache Valley, the beautiful country which the Utes had just given up. So we decided to go and have a look down there first. We bought a 3-inch Schuttler waggon and a pair of capital mules, Jack and Tom, and laying in a good camp-outfit and stock of provisions we started out.

Our route was not quite the same as that I had been over with Matthews, for Lew took the mountain road straight up into South Park, a wonderful natural basin in the mountains, some thirty miles across, and 9000 to 10,000 feet high. The buffalo had all been killed out from it except for one bunch still running on Tarryall, one of the side creeks off the Park ; but we saw nothing of these animals. What we did see along the road, as we made our way on to the Arkansas and then to the San Luis Park, was a fine buggy, with Major Bennett, the Indian Agent. He was on his way to Denver with Shawano and Wolf, two of the Ute chiefs, whom I had seen at Los Pinos, the year before. We just passed the time of day with them and went on, and finally we got to Saguache Creek,

which we hoped would prove our garden of Eden. It was good enough for most men even if it didn't quite come up to that. Glorious bunch and buffalo grass everywhere, steep-sided cañons here and there for shelter, pine timber for fuel and for building, a splendid trout river for fishing, for watering stock, and for irrigation, and miles and miles of natural hay meadows. What could the heart of a cattleman want more?

But, like every other Eden I ever heard of, ours had a snake in it, and old Godfrey, who remembered all about Matthews and myself last year, rubbed it well into us about the snake.

"You'll have to look out for the Utes," said Godfrey to us, when we told him we had decided to locate our ranch somewhere up the Saguache. "There are three hundred of them hunting deer up there now. They've hunted there all their lives. Of course Ouray, the head chief, has signed a treaty to move them across the Cochetopa range to Los Pinos, but these Winnemuches here under Shawano and Wolf are kind of mutinous against Ouray. They say they've hunted in these hills all their lives, and they ain't happy over the idea of being moved out."

"Oh," said Lew, "the Utes are friendly; I've been among them before. And, anyway, they ain't going to bother us just now, for we met Shawano and Wolf in a buggy in South Park; they've gone to Denver with Major Bennett, the agent, to interview Governor McCook."

"Well, mebbe you're right," said old Godfrey. "But keep your eyes skinned, that's all."

And so next day we drove our waggon up the cañon of the Saguache; the cañon was all right as a road; the bottom of it was grass land half a mile wide, with the river winding through it, and the side walls though perpendicular were only a hundred feet or so in height; a few miles up we passed the Ute camp, some sixty lodges, picturesquely grouped among the willows. We didn't stop to pay them a call, but a splendid-looking buck with silver plates all over his horse trappings came galloping out to interview us. Some of the Utes spoke a little Spanish and English, and my partner could generally make out to converse with them after a fashion.

" Where you go with waggon? " asked the Indian. Ours was nearly the first waggon that ever went up the Saguache, the Agency waggons excepted.

" Oh, just up the creek a bit," said Lew.

" What you do there? " persisted the red man. My partner explained that we were going to put up a ranch, and stock the range with cattle and so forth. The Indian listened silently.

" Why don't you do the same? " concluded Ed. " Try a little honest work for a change, and take to cattle raising for a living. It's the finest life out."

The red man curled his lips with disdain. " Navajo work," he said, " that all right. Mexican work, that all right for him. American work, all right too." He paused and ran a scornful eye over our farm waggon and team of mules. " Ute, no," he said. " Ute fight; kill men." And the son of the desert wheeled his spotted pony, put

the whip to his sides, and galloped off as quick as he had come.

"That's the real unadulterated Injun of it," commented Lew. "His one idea is to take scalps. But they know that it won't be healthy for 'em if they start in to attack the whites ; Ouray wouldn't allow 'em to do it nohow. He's been to Washington, and he knows our power. Some of the Utes wanted to fight us about the cession of Wet Mountain Valley, but he told 'em 'twasn't no use to kick. Says he to 'em : ' The white men have got a man for every tree.' " I had heard that before, but I did not tell Lew so.

So we moved up the Saguache and selected the site for our homestead, and spent three days cutting house logs and drawing them to the spot and putting up a log-cabin to hold our claim while we went back to bring in stores and a herd of cattle. We had finished our cabin, and on the third morning I was washing up the things after breakfast while Ed put on the harness, when there came two Indians riding through the ford lickity split, their horses' legs making the water fly in showers. They reined up abruptly at the edge of our camp and jabbered at us loud and fast.

"What are they saying ? " said I to Lew anxiously.

"Can't quite make 'em out," he answered. I could see that he was making an effort to restrain his voice and that he was not less anxious than myself.

"They're mad about something," he said, after

listening to them for a minute, " but what it is I don't know. They want us to shift, that's clear, and I guess we'd better lose no time. I wish we was safe down to Godfrey's."

The Indians wheeled their ponies and dashed off. We climbed on to the waggon seat and started the mules at a walk. Presently we saw lots of mounted Indians coming up the cañon, each man with his long rifle across the saddle in front of him. They were in little groups, two or three together. As we drew near them, instead of riding up in a friendly way to say " How," each group in turn left the trail and rode wide of us, with sour looks and averted faces. We grew more and more anxious.

Presently an Indian dropped behind one of the groups that had not yet turned out to avoid us, and dismounted to arrange his cinch or something. When we got to where he was he held up his hand, and my partner pulled up.

" What's all this fuss about ? " asked Lew.

" You know Wolf ? " asked the Indian. " You know Shawano ? " He spoke rather good English for a Ute.

" Yes," said my partner. " Met 'em a few days back in Bayou Salade [1] going to Denver to see Governor."

" Soldiers in Bayou Salade," said the Indian, " heap soldiers."

" Are there ? " said Lew. " Maybe so, but we ain't seen 'em."

" Soldiers in Bayou Salade," repeated the Indian,

[1] South Park.

" fight with Indian. Heap shoot." Then he made
a most expressive gesture with his right hand by
drawing it swiftly across his throat from ear to
ear. " Wolf—ugh," he said, indicating that the
chief had had his throat cut. " Shawano—ugh."
He did that expressive throat-cutting sign again.
" Utes give Americans hell," he said, " you get ! "
And with that he sprang on his pony and dashed
after his companions.

I looked at Lew, and I wondered if my face was
as grey as his. Probably it was.

We were in a trap, and we knew it.

Behind us stretched a thousand miles of wild
mountains all the way to California—there was
no escape that way. On either side rose the cañon
walls, and a man on foot let alone a pair of mules
and a waggon cannot climb a hundred feet of smooth
perpendicular rock. Before us lay the road we
had come, now swarming with redskins. We knew
the grim code of the red man, a life for a life. The
killing of Shawano and Wolf would be bloodily
avenged.

" Shall I get out the rifles ? " said I. The rifles
lay in the waggon bed at our feet.

" No," said he. " There's too many of 'em to
be bluffed, and if they've made up their minds
to go on the war-path the sight of the rifles would
be an extra temptation to 'em to begin. Our
one chance is that the Injuns won't begin till they've
hidden their squaws far up in the mountains. That's
a principle with them, and they're sure taking
'em off to hide now ; here they come."

A great band of Indian women, driving a herd of pack ponies on which were tied lodges and lodge poles and piles of buffalo robes and camp truck, rode past us on the left.   One of the women screeched frantically as she went by ; she was like one possessed by a fury, and would have rushed at us, but that the others restrained her ; to my horror I saw her face streaming with blood from a multitude of cuts.

" What has she been doing to herself ? " I exclaimed to Lew.

" Mourning for the dead," he answered briefly, " that's the way a squaw shows her sorrow when her buck's killed. She'll be Shawano or Wolf's squaw, sure."

Behind the squaws came the rearguard, forty or fifty Indians riding together. They did not turn out of the trail as we approached, but spread out on either side in a half moon and one in the centre held up his hand to stop us. We stopped.

" Where you go ? " he inquired, and his manner was not reassuring.

" Down to Godfrey's," answered Lew nonchalantly.

Scared as we both were I could not but admire the way in which he acted the part of a man entirely at his ease. He sat there leaning forward holding the reins loosely, whip in hand, the picture of a comfortable ranchman.

" What you do here ? " asked the red man.

Lew explained our business, and instantly there arose a warm debate amongst the Indians. We could not understand their words, but their mean-

ing was plain enough. They had us absolutely at their mercy, and half of them wanted to seize us and torture us right there. Their mercy! I looked at the ring of savage faces, and saw small signs of mercy on any of them. The wild man is ruthless as the wild beast, and those fierce, dark eyes that were bent upon us had no more pity in them than if they had been the eyes of a pack of wolves about to spring on the prey. I looked at the sun shining brightly in the blue sky and at the beautiful earth around, and I thought that I had never loved them half so much. We never know how much we love a thing till we lose it for ever; this might well be my last look, for fifty rifles were pointing my way.

Happily for us amongst these fierce savages were prudent ones, who urged delay. The ring in front of us suddenly opened, leaving a clear road through. The Indian who had spoken to us before said:

"You go Godfrey's, good. Not go beyond. Stay there"; and he pointed down the cañon.

I gave a sigh of relief.

"Keep your nerve up," whispered Lew, raising the reins and giving the mules a flick with the whip. "Git up thar', you Jack, you Tom," he drawled; and the mules bent to their work, and the waggon went on.

We passed through the ranks of our enemies.

"Don't look round," said my partner in an undertone. "Don't give 'em the least idea as we're scared of 'em."

So I refrained from turning my head; nevertheless, as we drew clear of them I had a horrid sensation as of a hailstorm of lead crashing into my back. How slow those mules went! They fairly seemed to crawl. Yard by yard, however, we drew away, and still no bullets came. Presently we were out of rifle shot, and I ventured to glance backwards. The Indians were moving on up the cañon. If only they did not repent and come galloping hot foot after us.

" Couldn't we go a little faster ? " said I.

" Wait till we're out of sight round the point," he said. Lew was a cool hand in a tight place.

A quarter of a mile farther we rounded the point, and I looked back again.

" Are they clean out of sight now ? " he asked.

" Yes," said I, " we've seen the last of 'em, I do hope."

Snap went the black snake whip, and the startled Jack and Tom sprang into their collars with a will. Ed braced his feet against the footboard, tightened the reins, and freely laid the whip on them, and away we flew. I'll warrant no pair of mules with a waggon behind them ever covered the ten miles that lay between us and Godfrey's in shorter time. The sweat ran off them like rain when at last we pulled up before his ranch. Godfrey came running out.

" Well, I'm darned glad to see you," he exclaimed. " I was afraid they'd finished you fellers this time."

" What's it all mean ? " asked Lew. " What's really happened ? "

" I'll tell you all I know," said Godfrey. " Three
o'clock this morning I was waked by being yanked
out of bed on to the floor and finding myself in
the middle of a mob of Indians with their knives
out ready to cut me up in small pieces. Shawano's
brother was the leader of 'em, so I sung out to
him to know what the devil it was all about. He
told me some story about Shawano and Wolf having their throats cut by the soldiers. ' Rot,' says
I to him. ' Who ladled you out all that hog-
wash ? ' ' Jim,' they all cried. ' Jim was there,
and he says it's true.' ' Jim's a liar,' says I. ' Jim's
a liar, and you know it.' "

Jim was the name given by the whites to one
of the Ute chiefs.

" Well, that kind of took 'em aback. They
hadn't thought of that before. But they acknow-
ledged the corn ; they all do know Jim for a liar.
So they let go of me—they had me down on the
floor—and I got up and sat on the bed and pala-
vered 'em a bit. Did Ouray know about this ?
' No,' they said. ' Ouray was away at Costilla,
and he didn't know.' ' Very well,' says I, ' you'll
have Ouray in your wool if you touch a hair of
any white man's head without his leave. He's
the boss chief. If you go to war without his leave
he'll give you what for. You send a runner and
ask him what he thinks first.'

" They agreed to that—they knew themselves
they'd orter have done it already and they sent
off a runner at oncet. Then I went at 'em again.
' Where did Jim say this happened ? ' I asked.

' Bayou Salade,' they answered. ' And how was it his throat wasn't cut too ? ' says I. ' Oh, he wasn't there with them himself,' they said. ' He was close by, and heard the soldiers shout, and some Mexicans who were there with bull teams told him the soldiers had cut the throats of the other two and were going to cut his. So he ran all the way across the mountains to tell us.' ' Ran seventy-five miles afoot,' says I, ' because of some lying bull-whacker's story. You're a sweet-scented lot, aren't you, to let yourselves be greened in that way.'

" And I just rubbed it into them what fools they were. So the upshot was that they've agreed to do nothing till they've heard from Ouray, and till another couple of runners they've sent off to South Park to inquire after the health of the murdered men have come back. Till then it's to be peace. Meanwhile we white men here in Saguache have fixed it up to hang together, and if it is war we'll put up a lively fight right here. And I'm mighty glad to have you two fellers to help us."

Lew and I were equally glad to be alive to help. The house was loop-holed and put in a state of defence, and three long anxious days we waited there, expecting the issues of peace or war. The Utes hid their women in the mountains and then came back and surrounded the little settlement a hundred strong, strutting about as if they already were masters of us and of our scalps. Shawano's brother took a particular fancy to mine. My hair in those days was long and curling, and in frontier fashion I had let it grow down to my shoulders.

It would have made a lovely scalp, and time and again I caught the greedy eyes of the bloodthirsty redskin fixed on it with a covetous glare.

But my curly locks never went to adorn his bridle reins. On the fourth day came a tired pony galloping heavily into Saguache with two buck Indians on his back. They sprang to the ground, and then what warm greetings and congratulations followed! The two were Shawano and Wolf, alive and unharmed. The pipe of peace was speedily passed round and all was well. Godfrey had divined the trouble exactly. Nothing whatever had happened to them; but a malicious lying Mexican hearing the soldiers shouting had thought it fun to give Jim a fright, and Jim, a liar himself, and credulous as all liars are, had straightway run back to the Ute camp and started all this trouble. Now, however, he ran from the camp to hide from Shawano, and well he might, for Shawano was an angry man. The squaw with her face all cut to pieces was his squaw. She had mourned for him properly. She had gashed her face cruelly with sharp flints, she had burned his lodge, she had broken his bow and killed his war pony; in short, she had done everything that befitted the widow of a great warrior. But it was rough on Shawano, who wasn't dead at all. Jim did well to hide, for Shawano swore he would kill him whenever he caught him. I sincerely hope he did.

Wolf and I made great friends. He spoke quite a little English, and he greatly appreciated my Sharpe's 50-calibre rifle when I showed it to him.

It was about the best rifle going in 1870, and he begged me to let him try it. As we were all dear friends now I consented and gave him some cartridges to try what he could do with it. Just then, I was at the most exciting part in a novel I had found in Godfrey's house, and I went on with my book instead of going outside to see Wolf's performance, though of course I heard the shots. Presently in ran Wolf, much pleased with himself, and dragged me away from my story to see what he had done. Sure enough he had stuck up a card on a tree trunk close by, and he had put three or four shots on to the card and one within half an inch of the spade-ace which was the bull's-eye.

" Now you," he urged, trying to make me take the rifle. " You shoot."

" Oh," I returned, " I don't want to be bothered. I know just how it shoots. Rifle's all right. No use to waste ammunition."

" No," persisted the eager Indian. " You shoot ! You shoot ! "

And to please him I did.

Up came the rifle to my shoulder. Quick I glanced down the sights and squeezed the trigger. Bang ! The card fell off the tree and fluttered to the ground. I had driven up the nail through the middle of the spade-ace which fastened it to the tree.

Wolf fairly fell upon my neck.

" Oh," he sighed, " you come with me. Come with me out on the Plains and kill Kiowas."

That was the Ute's idea of Paradise, being able to kill Kiowas. But I hadn't lost any Kiowas.

CHAPTER IX

THE EXPANDING BEAN

NO, I hadn't lost any Kiowas, neither had Lew and I lost any Utes. The fact was, our Ute scare had rather put both him and me off the notion of taking up that Saguache ranch. Lew had two women to think of, and the mere thought of the awful position of the two Godfrey women when those Utes held us there in the hollow of their hand was enough. True, the Plains Indians, if they ever got hold of you and yours, were every bit as bad, but then their range was fifty times the size of the Utes': they had the whole of the great Buffalo range, the Plains, to wander in, about a million of square miles: that allowed all parties a little elbow room, and, with any luck, one might settle on the Plains and never see an Indian.

So Lew and I made tracks back to Denver again, where we joined up with his friend, Ex-Governor A. C. Hunt, and with him we went out on the Plains south of the Divide to look for another site for a ranch. Hunt told us he knew of a place that he thought would do for us, and he took us there all right. It was on the head of Black Squirrel Creek, one of the many dry creeks running south

from the Divide to the Arkansas. The spot we pitched on lay about twelve miles south of the Bijou Basin and ten miles from the great pine forest that covered the top of the Divide. Forty miles away to the west stood Pike's Peak, its glorious red granite dome towering 14,000 feet into the sky, over double the height of our ranch, which was but some 6,000 odd. We were fifty miles due north of the Arkansas River, thirty miles east of that Manitou Spring I had already visited, and twenty-five miles east of the place on Fountain Creek where Colorado Springs was afterwards built. You could locate it by these bearings on the map in a moment.

The reason we chose this place was that out here on the dry Plains, two fine springs of pure, clear water gushed out and fed a series of pools for over a quarter of a mile below. These pools had been a favourite drinking-place for the buffalo, and the bare bones of their old skeletons lay bleaching about. We did not see any live ones, but we knew that if we wanted to we should not have far to go. Antelope were all round there in herds ; the country was open and rolling, not very unlike our English downs, and it was covered with abundance of buffalo grass and bunch grass, the best possible feed for stock. Half a mile south from the springs were some 50 acres of a much heavier and stronger grass, a real natural hay meadow. This we called the vega, the Spanish word for meadow ; hay grass grew here because the soil was damp, being watered from below, doubtless from the same subterranean source that fed our two springs. Here we took up

claims ; Lew and Hunt knew all about the land business, which was a thing that I did not understand much about, and so very naturally I left that part of the business to them. Then back we went to Denver, where we said good-bye to Governor Hunt. Then Lew and I got a mowing-machine and hay-rake, and also bought two half-broken bronco mares from the California herd of Billy and Hi Ford, the men who had sold me Methusalem. One, a roan, was called Molly, and the other, a brown, we named Betty. These broncos were to prove an unlucky purchase for me, for I had parted with the steady and quiet Methusalem some time before, as he was a bit old and slow. Lew now took his brother Jud away from his employment to come and help us, and he drove the hay-rake with the Jack mule out to the ranch while Lew, who very justly fancied himself as a driver, hitched the bronco mares to the waggon and drove them.

Arrived at the ranch site we pitched our tent, but we did not want to go wasting time in building a cabin as the hay season was getting on, so we instantly went to putting up hay : Lew drove the bronco mares in the mower while Jud and I raked and pitched the hay and carried it with the mules and waggon to the stack by the springs. We had no neighbours ; our nearest was old man Russell, a jovial, elderly Irishman with a family, who had a small herd of American cows which he milked and herded with the aid of a wonderful old Mexican who rejoiced in the name of Katarina.

Russell's ranch was eight miles from us, close

to the timber on the Divide and not far from Weir's sawmill. East of us there were no settlers at all for hundreds of miles, not until you got far over the western line of Kansas. In between us and them were the Plains, where the wild buffalo and the even wilder red men still held their own.

The three of us shared the camp work fairly enough, but Lew kept all the handling of the bronco-mares to himself, for he was skilful with horses, and the wild brutes did take some management; thus, a good deal of the cooking fell to my share. The importance of cooking was a thing I quite rose to. I had noticed that Governor Hunt was a life-long victim to dyspepsia, and in order to get something he could eat safely he did most of his own cooking in camp, and it had been much the same with the wretched Matthews, who was a confirmed dyspeptic too. But the three of us, the two Howells and myself, were young men, and we had absolutely unimpaired digestions, while hard work made us as hungry as wolves. Generally we feasted on ante-lope meat, for I was nearly always out after antelope with my rifle, whenever I wasn't called on to perform with a pitchfork. When antelope failed, we fell back on bacon.

Lew himself was, as he expressed it, " no slouch of a camp cook; " and under his vigorously sar-castic tuition I learned before long to make splendid coffee, to bake capital bread in a Dutch oven, to boil a potato properly, and to slice and fry the sow-belly, as he chose to call the bacon. In preparing this last dish Lew's ideas were really quite artistic :

he taught me to put the rashers on a tin plate when they were done, and then to mix smoothly a heaped spoonful of flour into the sizzling hot fat in the frying-pan and brown it ; to this, by his instructions, I added a cupful of hot water and stirred the mess till it thickened into a rich gravy, which gave a most excellent relish to our plain butterless bread and potatoes. The name he gave this savoury sauce was rather too coarse to print, but that didn't prevent it from tasting mighty good. The potatoes, as I found, must be neither sodden nor underdone, while experience showed me that the large ones took longer to boil than the small, and that if I served them up while still hard inside I was liable to draw down not only the sarcasms of my partner but also the avenging furies of dyspepsia.

Finally my vaulting ambition as a cook soared to beans. One morning I had to stay in camp with a lame foot, while Lew and his brother vanished over the hill to cart hay in the vega. " I'll give them a real treat for dinner to-day," said I to myself, as the thought of beans entered my mind. More than once I had heard my partner sing the praises of " frijoles," or Mexican brown beans, but he had never got out any to cook, though I knew we had a whole sackful of them in the outfit. Accordingly I rummaged round till I got hold of the sack, untied it, and filled up the iron pot in which I usually boiled the potatoes with a quantity of innocent-looking little shiny hard brown beans not quite so large as hazel-nuts. I poured in water enough just to cover the beans, exactly as I had learned

to do with potatoes, and I set the pot by the camp fire to boil. It did occur to me that I was setting about a novel enterprise, but I recollected a chance remark of Lew's, " You can't overboil a bean," so I thought it no harm to be on the safe side and give them plenty of time. That done, I hunted up a novel and lay down on my blankets to enjoy the unwonted luxury of a book. After some twenty minutes I got up to have a look at the beans, and see if they were not pretty near done, as my limited experience told me would have been the case with potatoes. I was not a little surprised to find a sort of mushroom formation protruding from the pot, consisting of a mass of beans crowned on top by the pot-lid, which had risen up several inches. Also, when I came to examine, I couldn't perceive any sign of water in the pot. " Very odd," thought I. " Where can it have all gone to ? Potatoes never act like that. Well, anyway, if these things want more room I'll give them another show." So I got out our other iron pot, removed half the beans into it, filled both up with water, and went back to have a second spell at my novel. After a quarter of an hour I went to look again, and lo ! by this time two overblown swollen protuberances had formed themselves, the two pot-lids had been heaved on high like the first, and once more all the water had mysteriously disappeared.

I searched round for another cooking vessel and found nothing more available than the big coffee pot, so I carefully rinsed it out, and patiently redistributed the beans once more, and after filling up

all three pots with water replaced them by the fire. Looking again after another quarter of an hour, I found three great fat mushrooms protruding from the three pots. This was past bearing. Almost desperate, I snatched up our tin dipper and filled that with those maddening beans! To cut the story short, when Lew and his brother came back from the hayfield they found the camp fire ringed all round with every single utensil we possessed that would hold water down to empty peach-cans, and every single one was as full of beans as it could hold, and they were swelling still. Talk of a bean-feast!

How Lew and Jud did shout! I thought they would never have done laughing as I shyly explained that I thought you boiled beans like potatoes, only longer, and I was not allowed to forget that bean-feast in a hurry!

" This your first introduction to the gay and festive bean ? " mocked Lew. " Guess you'll remember after this the way them little jokers act. They all do it, too, all them dry vittles like rice and beans and dried apples. Why, a half-pint of dried apples'll go on taking in water till a bushel measure won't hold 'em. You didn't never stop at a boarding-house back East, I reckon ? " Lew had the Western man's sovereign contempt for his fellow-citizens who were unfortunate enough to be born near the Atlantic coastline.

" No," said I, " never. You know I came practically straight here from the old country."

" Ah," said he. " Then you missed something.

Why, at some of them down East boarding-houses, where they're just mean enough to skin a flea for his hide an' tallow, their bill-of-fare is dried apples for breakfast, warm water for dinner, and let-'em-swell for supper.   But we don't do that sort of way out West.''

It was more than once or twice that I repented of having parted with Methusalem. Slow and old he may have been, but he was as tame as a dog, and that for one like myself was simply an invaluable quality. Those two broncos, Molly and Betty, were a continual nuisance. Lew Howell was a good driver and a handy man, but he was not a born horse-tamer. He handled the broncos coolly and well, but he had none of the sympathetic, I had almost said hypnotic, power which men who have the gift of it cast like a spell over animals. Such men are found among all races in all countries, but they are none too common anywhere. The result in our case was that though Lew worked the pair of mares every day in the mowing-machine, they remained kittle cattle, while the mules with which Jud and I raked and carted the hay were quiet enough. One day while Jud was raking with the Jenny mule and I was busy with the pitchfork making the haycocks, I heard a shout from Lew, who was mowing quite close to where I was. I turned sharp, dropping the fork, and my very first thought was, " Where's my rifle ? " Always at the back of our minds was, as it were, an alarm signal set and ready to ring : a surprise attack by Cheyennes or Arapahoes was the thing we ever-

lastingly watched out for. But there was no Arapahoe scare this journey! What I instantly perceived was that Madam Molly, the off mare, had gone into one of her abominable ugly tantrums and had got her near hind-leg over the tongue or pole of the mower, and there she was almost down, throwing herself about in the fierce effort to get herself clear. Without stopping to think, I dashed at her to grab hold of her head and get her up and off the tongue, never realizing that the mower was still in gear and moving forward by jerks, so that when I sprang to seize hold of Molly I was placing myself in front of those awful teeth on the scythe bar. Just what did happen I can't remember : but I must have fallen somehow and those teeth tore my right leg horribly before Lew could throw the machine out of gear, and get the Betty mare to stop pulling, and so bring the whole affair to a stop. I believe I fainted with the pain. What I do know is that he and Jud somehow pulled me clear, and stopped the flow of blood, and tied up my wounds, and carried me into camp. Most frontiers-men had a rough skill in surgery in those days. But more than that was wanted for my hurts, which were pretty serious, and the end was that I must go to Denver where there were surgeons. Accordingly Lew remained in camp alone to go ahead with the hay as best he might, while Jud took me in the waggon to Denver. They half-filled the waggon-bed with hay to make it ride easier for me, nevertheless sixty-five miles in a springless waggon with a horrible leg like mine

is not exactly jam. However, I made it through somehow ; Dr. Justice, a capital man who had been a war surgeon and knew all about wounds, fixed me up good ; and Mrs. Howell and her daughter nursed me not inefficiently in their way. Thus it came about that I spent the latter part of the summer of 1870 either in my bed or else hobbling about Denver with a very lame leg. But the splendid pure air of Colorado and the skill of Dr. Justice cured me after a while. I remember looking at the scars on my leg when I was nearly right again and saying to the doctor, " When will those marks go away ? " " Not till the worms eat 'em," he grinned back. He was a true American, and their humour is a bit dry sometimes. When I told Dr. Justice how my accident had occurred, he said : " Oh, yes, you were just a little bit startled. I remember I was startled once myself down below here on the Platte when I was coming out across the Plains. I hoofed it the whole 500 miles across, getting my truck carried on a bull-waggon. One morning the bulls were missing, and I went out to help hunt 'em up as well as the bull-whacker himself. I was looking in the brush down by the river when I plumped right on to a hidden Indian. He was lying there dead still, but he jumped like a cat when I nearly trod on him ; he had his bow and arrows ready, and he got three arrows loosed off at me before I could reach for my gun. I'll allow I was startled. Luckily he was startled too, for his three arrows didn't get home on me, only one of 'em stuck in my overcoat, and in about three

seconds I managed to get my ·44-calibre Colt up level and squeeze her off. Down went Mr. Indian. Guess he was worse startled still that time. But for those three seconds I did think it was a case of Kingdom-come."

Yes, I liked Dr. Justice first-rate, for his stories as well as his surgery. Both were good enough for me.

CHAPTER X

MY RUNNING FIGHT

LEW came in to Denver with the waggon from the ranch, to find me completely mended up. We went round town together to see our friends, and right there in Gus Cheever's office we ran on to a man who had for sale just the very thing we thought we wanted next, namely, a bunch of cattle.

The owner of the cattle was Major Oakes, and he had them down at a ranch some way off on the Platte where they were kept. I rather think the ranchman had them on the shares; that was a common arrangement in those days. We went down there with the Major and we liked the cattle; they certainly seemed all right, and we bought the lot. They were American cattle, that is to say, the same breed as our English dairy stock, quite unlike the tall, gaunt, long-horned Spanish stock that came from Texas which were now pouring into Southern Colorado. There were about fifty of them and the cows were broke gentle to milk; the head of the herd was old Charley, a big white bull with red ears, the same colour as the wild white cattle of Chillingham, and many of the calves and young stock took their markings from him. We

also took over a bay cow-pony who as well as the bull was called Charley. Both the pony and these American cattle were perfectly quiet, so much so that Lew and I settled to take them straight down over the Divide to the ranch, he driving the waggon and I herding the cattle along.

We got them to the ranch safe enough, and there turned them loose, and they made themselves quite at home and grazed all over the splendid pasture on the range, which was new to them.

I felt quite proud of my performance in having brought them along, and I began to think myself a regular cowpuncher.

The hay had been stacked by Lew and Jud, and before Lew came in to find me in Denver they had put up a sixteen-foot-square log-cabin alongside the spring. Now the two of them went up on the Divide into the timber to cut house logs to build a proper ranch house to bring his mother and sister out to, while I lived all alone by myself in the cabin, hunting antelope and seeing that the cattle did not stray off the range. Also I had to take care of the broncos, Molly and Betty, for Lew took the mules, Jack and Tom, to haul the logs with. Every few days Lew would bring down a load of logs, just to see that I was all right with the cattle, and then take back a load of antelope meat which he could trade off at Weir's Mill.

Of course I found it a little bit of a strain living so much alone.

Eastward for five hundred miles stretched the undulating swells of what the maps used to call

the Great American Desert, an empty wilderness tenanted only by the wild buffalo and antelope and the wilder red men who hunted them.

Thirteen men had been scalped the previous spring within forty miles of where we had settled, and naturally I was on the look-out for the Indians night and day. As I roamed around over the prairie I watched for the tracks of their unshod ponies on the sandy soil, or scanned the horizon for the sight of a band of these roving marauders. It seemed to me in my solitude that there was but a step between me and the most horrible of deaths. I was living on the Ragged Edge. I know no better phrase than that to express the everlasting tension of the nerves under such conditions.

I had more than one false alarm. Both cattle and antelope, travelling to water on a hot day in single file, are often so transfigured by the " smoke " or mirage caused by the currents of heated air rising from the surface of the ground that they look very like a line of horsemen.

The flickering, wavering effect of this " smoke " distorts the shapes and sizes of things amazingly. Objects seen through it are blurred and broken, like the reflections in still water when the ripples from an oar cross them. A soapweed half a mile away will look for a minute like a tall man walking, and then change and look like an antelope or a wolf, and presently change again into what it really is, a big weed.

The constant changes baffle and confuse the eye. One believes, and disbelieves, and believes again ;

but, no matter how often one may have been deceived, one can never know if next time may not be the grim reality. Your eye suddenly falls on what seem to be Indians, and your heart leaps to your mouth ; there is no better phrase than that to express the sudden start and the tightening of the chest when the eye discerns something which it takes to be a merciless foe close at hand.

"There they are !" you say, and brace yourself for a struggle against fearful odds or a race for life. You wait for a minute, breathless, expecting your fate. Then the mirage shifts, or the objects come nearer.

"It's only that bunch of cows, with the black muley in the lead," you say to yourself, and all the imaginary struggle and race for life that filled your mind vanishes like the mirage.

One morning I was out as usual after the cattle. I missed a bunch of them from their wonted haunts, and put spurs to my pony and set off in a hurry to find out what had become of them.

As I galloped around, looking for my stray cattle, I came to the top of a rise in the prairie. Instantly I pulled my pony up short, and looked ahead hard, for there, down in a hollow, were my cattle ; and there among them was a horseman.

He sat quite still on his horse and looked at me, as I did at him. He was some three hundred yards away, and it was not easy for either of us to make out what the other was. My figure, being outlined sharply against the sky, must have given him an advantage here.

My heart was in my mouth in a moment. Was

I at last face to face with one of the dreaded red men ? He wore a hat, but an Indian was quite capable of putting one on as a disguise. Yet certainly on the whole he did seem very like a white man.

But before I could make up my mind, he had jumped off his horse and lain down on the ground flat on his face, and as he jumped off I could see that he was wearing cowboy " shaps." My relief was immediate and great. He was a cowboy of course.

" But what on earth's the man up to ? " said I to myself. " That's a foolish trick for a man to play—to get off his horse on the prairie, right among the cattle ! "

Prairie cattle, though perfectly used to mounted men, are generally very much disturbed and excited by the sight of a man on foot, and are likely to make a rush at him. To dismount in the midst of them a man must have a strong reason.

I watched him more closely than ever. Suddenly from the prostrate figure came a puff of smoke. I heard the crack of a rifle and ping-g-g of a bullet whizzing past me.

" What ! " said I to myself. " He's shooting at me ! I must run quick and explain—no time to lose about it, either."

Touching spurs to my pony, I rode at him as hard as I could go, shouting out, " Hold on ! hold on ! "

He didn't hold on at all. He sprang up from the ground and upon his horse, and rode away like the wind. I followed him, still trying to explain, and yelling " Hold on ! " at the top of my voice.

But the more I shouted the more he ran. My pony was fast, and I gained on him. Then I saw him cast a look behind him, and leaning forward in the saddle, raise his right hand and begin to belabour his horse's sides with his quirt, as if more than anxious to get away as fast, and as far, as he could.

Then it dawned upon my delighted brain that the man mistook me for an Indian! I halloed to him to stop, and to come and see me at home, and dine and sleep. But no; he only took my hallos for war-whoops, and plied the whip harder than ever.

I was very young in those days, and my great ambition was to qualify as a regular out-and-out frontiers-man. In order to get my face well tanned, I wore on my head, instead of a wide-brimmed cowboy hat, nothing but a little round cap; it was practically the same thing as having none at all. My hair had grown long, and hung down almost to my shoulders. Furthermore, as I used to walk considerable distances after antelope, I wore light shoes, like moccasins, instead of the high boots with the trousers tucked in, after the universal fashion of the frontier. I had no beard, and it may be easily believed that with my bronzed smooth face, bare head, and long hair, I must really have looked, at a distance, extremely like an Indian. But we kept no looking-glass on the ranch, so that this fact had never occurred to me till that moment.

At last I gave up the chase in despair, and reined in on the brow of a wide sand gulch, which wound

for miles away through the prairie. Down. the steep side of it he plunged ; I saw the sand fly in showers from his horse's heels as he scurried across the gulch. Up the opposite side he dashed, and away over the broad flats which stretched beyond.

I must have watched him while he rode three miles ; and as far as the eye could follow he was keeping the horse at its fastest pace. Evidently he was badly scared—" stampeded," in fact.

I am afraid I must confess that when I gave up the chase, I had, boy-like, to give a whoop or two that might have passed muster as an Arapahoe yell. It tickled my fancy to have been under fire, and to have stampeded a real live cowboy, all by myself.

I returned to my cattle, which proved to be all right, and then betook myself as usual to trying to find antelope. I saw no more of the fugitive.

One evening, about a week afterwards, as I was picketing out my pony to graze after his day's work, I saw a man ride up to the cabin, and I recognized him as Pat Higgins, a sheep man from the Divide, whom I had once met riding round.

" Hallo ! " said I, coming towards him with the axe in my hand with which I had been driving the picket pin. " Is that you, Pat ? I'm glad to see you. Get off and look at your saddle ; and, if you think it would look better off too, strip it, and come in and stop for the night."

" Well," said he, slowly dismounting, " it's going on to camp I was, but indade it's a matther of twelve or fourteen miles further, and the baste's tired."

" Oh, come in," said I. " There's plenty of hay for your horse, or you can stake him out on green grass down by the spring there, alongside of mine, if you like."

" Tell me, now, wan thing," said he, as he took off his saddle and turned his horse loose to roll in the dust and then graze around. " Have ye seen any sthray work-oxen around here ? There's a big red stag with O. B. on his hip I'm looking for."

" No," I answered, " I haven't seen him. There aren't any strays with our cattle just now. But bring your saddle inside, so the wolves won't gnaw it, and I'll fry some antelope meat and have supper ready in a jiffy."

Pat came into the cabin and sat down on my best chair—an empty box, turned bottom upward.

" And tell me, now," he began, " where's yer folks ? Where's yer partner, and the Mexican ye had working for ye ? "

" Off up on the Divide getting out house logs."

Having cut up a frying-pan full of antelope steaks I set them on the fire.

It made me very cheerful to have any company at all, and Pat was a capital fellow. He looked at me now with a puzzled expression.

" But how do ye manage here at all ? " he inquired. " You don't mean to tell me that ye're living out here all alone by yourself ? "

" That's just what I am doing," I replied, " I'm alone here, hunting antelope and minding the stock."

" Murther ! " he exclaimed. " I wouldn't live alone like that out here for a hundred dollars a

month, not if ye paid me for it. Why now, aren't ye afeared of the Injuns? It's a wonder they haven't scalped ye."

"Well, I've kept my hair on, so far," laughed I, in the nervous way one laughs as a sort of relief over perils escaped.

"Then you've done more than I've done," returned Higgins, and putting his hands up to his head he proceeded to my great surprise to take off his hair. It was a wig that he wore. But what appeared when the wig was removed was not the bald shining dome one expected to see. Instead there was a strange-looking surface, too dreadful to describe.

"Oh, Great Scott!" I cried.

"The Sioux scalped me three years ago up yonder in Wyoming, beyond the Union Pacific," he said, in a matter-of-fact tone, "but, the way I look at it, to be scalped once in a lifetime is more than enough for any man, and that's why I wouldn't live out here alone the way you do for a hundred dollars a month."

"But," I rejoined, "you go on living in this country all the same. I wonder you don't go and live back in the States. Isn't there any danger there, where you are?"

"Och, not much at all," he answered. "What ud I want to go back to the States for? I'm kind of wonted out here on the frontier. Sure, there's a good many ranches round where I live, and 'tis safe enough I feel there. But out here 'tis too lonesome. I call ut nothing less than a merricle how you've escaped."

" Oh, well," said I, " I'm always on the look-out, of course, that's one thing. And then, too, you see there haven't been any in here this year—at least not nearer than Big Sandy."

Pat opened his eyes wide.

" Is that what ye think ? " he cried. " This prairie was runnin' over full of Injuns only last week, and however ye kept yer hair I can't tell."

" What ? " I almost shouted, jumping up excitedly from the pan, where I was turning the slices of meat with a fork. " Indians in here last week ? Why, I've been all about on the prairie every day, and keeping a sharp look-out, too, for tracks, and I've never seen a sign of them."

" Tracks, or no tracks, they was right in here on Big Horse Creek—a band of about twenty-five bloodthirsty Cheyennes on the war-path. Jim Smart, one of Van Schuyler's herders up here lookin' for cattle, ran on to 'em in the hills over east toward the head of Big Sandy, and had a running fight with 'em for twenty miles. He says they chased him pretty close, but he killed five of 'em that he knows on. His horse was just about clean give out when he got back to the camp at Crow's Roost."

Naturally I was much excited by this piece of news. Hostile Indians on my range ! My little cabin was easily visible from the hills over toward Big Sandy. How had they failed to see it, to creep up to it, shoot and scalp me, and run off the horses ?

I could not understand how I escaped.

" Yes," continued Pat, looking meditatively at the frying meat, " Jim must have had a terrible

time of it, sure.   He's a brave man, and no mistake.
I'll tell you what he says to me : ' I saw they was
too many for me,' says he, ' and I run my horse a
bit till I had 'em all strung out, and then I hops
off and shoots and drops the foremost wan, and
that sort of checks 'em a bit ; and then I hops on
agin, and takes my horse along easy till they begin
to crowd me agin, and then I hops off agin and drops
another ; and that way,' says he, ' I stood 'em off
till I got plumb back to camp.'   Och, now, it's himself that's a cool hand ! "

Something in the phrase " Hop off and shoot
and hop on again " roused my attention.   A sus-
picion flashed across me.   Could this hero be the
man ? No, it was impossible.   Still I was not satisfied.

" When did you say all this happened ? " I
asked.

" Why, the middle of last week," he answered,
" when Van Schuyler's outfit was camped down
here at Crow's Roost.   They've moved from there
since."

" Just the time when I had my little encounter
with the cowboy who got stampeded," thought I
to myself.

" And this man you speak of," I continued,
" ran on to the Indians in these hills over east
here ? "

" That's where he found 'em, or they found him,"
said Pat, " sure."

Another curious coincidence ! That was just
where I found my stray cattle, and that strange
horseman among them.

"And you say they ran him towards Crow's Roost?"

"That's what they did," said Patrick; "and if you'll hear me talk, you'll not stop here a day longer. It's too lonesome for ye intirely. Ye'd betther move yer stock at wance up on the Divide, where there's more settlers."

His advice fell upon unheeding ears. It was all as clear as daylight to me now. The last I had seen of my stampeded cowboy, he was heading for Crow's Roost as straight as he could go; and I understood very well that Jim Smart, Pat's heroic Indian fighter, was none other than my headlong runaway, and that I, by myself, was those "twenty-five bloodthirsty Cheyennes" and five of me was dead.

And here I should like to tell of a rather different sort of visitor that I entertained later on, one certainly not less quaint in his way than Pat. Out on the prairie I found a certain stray journalist who had lost himself there while looking for "copy." I took him home with me, warmed him, fed him, and gave him blankets to sleep in. He was truly grateful, and then proceeded to show his gratitude by turning me into "copy," wherein he gave a very free rein to his imagination. Here is what he produced:

"AN ENGLISH GENTLEMAN AS A RANCH-MAN.

"Richard B. Townshend, a younger son of Marquis Townshend, England, did not in his ancestral home contemplate with serenity or anticipate with

joy either of the lives of genteel aristocratic indigence prescribed by custom and tradition for the younger sons of noble English families. He had no desire to pass his life mounting guard and attending dress parade in an English garrison town or at a distant military post in Canada. Neither did he pant for military glory to be won beneath a tropical sun in the forests of Ashantee or the jungles of India. And he had no ambition to lead a life of humble piety as curate of a small parish with a smaller salary. So five or six years ago he gathered together what loose sovereigns he could and came to America, and finally found his way to Colorado, purchased a quarter section of land in El Paso county, about twenty-five miles east of Colorado Springs, and commenced raising stock and poultry and cultivating wheat and potatoes, and is independent and happy as an American sovereign. He says it is better to realize a good income from selling cattle and spring chickens and ranch eggs, early potatoes and onions, as a member of the great American Democracy, than it is to receive from an English lieutenancy or curacy a scanty salary as a member of the venerable British aristocracy.

" Mr. Townshend is a gentleman of thorough culture and large attainments, is a graduate of Trinity College, and he retains all his literary and scholarly tastes, and buys the latest book with the latest improved article for farm or domestic use. He lives in a log cabin with a mud roof, and does his own cooking, mixing with the flour and water,

and other ingredients that make the dough for his bread, discussions on art and science and literature. He is equally fluent of speech whether reading Homer or Virgil, in the ancient original, or conversing with his herders in our modern vernacular. But to be able to swear at an obstinate mule or a bucking bronco in several languages is of no special advantage. There are no oaths so effective as those expressed in our terse vigorous Saxon. Mr. Townshend, by his worth, ability, culture, genuine manliness and democracy, has won a deserved and a wide popularity."

I need hardly say that most of this stuff was made up. Most assuredly I did not tell him that I was any sort of relation to the Marquis Townshend. That was one thing he invented. And for another thing I did not raise chickens and potatoes like any small farmer up on the Divide or down on the Fountain. I was a real Colorado cattleman on a cow-ranch where I rode all day hunting cattle, where I lived in the saddle, and not a little proud I was of it. The small farmer's life did not attract me at all. But this good man wanted to be as nice to me as he knew how in return for what hospitality I had been able to show him ; so he just invented all that about the wheat and the hens and the rest, whatever he thought would be the most flattering details to please me, and he shoved them all in regardless.

CHAPTER XI

WOLVES AND CROWS

LEW and Jud went on cutting house logs and fence posts and fence poles up on the Divide, for we were going to have a real good barn for the horses and corrals for the cattle as well as a six-roomed log house for the family. Meantime my business was to keep an eye on our bunch of cattle and slay all the antelope I could. At Weir's Mill the meat got us sawn boards to line the corral and to make the floors of the house. I did my hunting on horseback now, getting off Charley and leaving him to graze, "tied to the ground," as the phrase was, by the reins being pulled over his head and dropped while I stalked the game on foot. And Charley being perfectly gentle I could also pack the meat home on him. At the ranch I kept the two bronco mares picketed, and I turned Charley loose nights to feed, knowing he would not go far from them.

And then one morning Charley turned up lame. Dead lame he was, and no error, and I couldn't in the least account for it. It wasn't the shoeing, for he was barefoot, of course, like all cow ponies in those days. Oh, how I wished Lew would turn up; he'd be sure to know; he knew such a lot about horses.

However, I had to do the best I could. Lew perhaps might come ; he came down every few days with a load of logs ; anyway, the cattle were certain to be all right, and I could go on hunting antelope afoot, which thing I accordingly proceeded to do. Carrying my heavy Sharp's rifle I walked out a long way towards the head of Big Sandy, and of course as I had no horse to ride the antelope were feeding much farther off that morning. I found a bunch at last, however, and in it was the very biggest buck I had seen yet, and I stalked him successfully and got in a shot. But my shot, alas, was not a good one, for I didn't drop him dead, but only crippled him so that he could just walk and couldn't run. I felt weak at the idea of packing him all that long way home, and it came to me as a happy thought to make him carry himself in. So I got round behind him and drove him towards the cabin. We came to a dry sand gulch about a mile from the ranch, and there he lay down and turned his head and looked at me with his beautiful liquid eyes like a gazelle's. I had grown somewhat callous. It doesn't cultivate the finer feelings much to live out on the Ragged Edge, to watch out day and night for wild men who will torture you to death if they can catch you, to lead a life scarcely less savage than that of a Red Indian. But the pathetic look of that poor brute went to my heart. I felt I could drive him no longer, so I raised my rifle and put him out of his pain. And then I made a great mistake : it was because I saw that he was so heavy and I was dog-tired.

What proved to be one of the most ill-omened ideas I ever had in my life came into my head. Why not make the half-broken mare, Molly, drag him in for me ?   I could saddle her up, that I knew, because in my presence she had been saddled and ridden by Jud Howell several times.   I did not propose to myself to get on her back, because I was quite aware that I was not a bronco-buster. Nor could I even hope to make her carry the carcass on her back, for I knew that, even if some bronco-busters might be able to do such a thing, for me it would be quite impossible to pack a dead antelope on the scary creature ;   but it suddenly flashed across my tenderfoot brain that I might bring her out and make her drag the carcass in by a rope fastened to the horn of the saddle.   True, I hadn't been long out in the West, and I had never happened to see the thing done, but I had often heard of it as a usual dodge.   So I walked to the cabin, got out the saddle, and by careful manœuvring I managed to put it on the mare and led her out to where the antelope lay.   I tied a rope to the antelope and made the other end of it fast to the saddle and then began to draw the cinch tighter, so that the saddle might stand the pull, when suddenly the vicious brute turned her head, saw what I was at, and let out savagely at me, breaking off a piece of the bone of my right leg below the knee.   Serve me right, you may say, for not having held on to the bridle while drawing the cinch ;   but I was only a tenderfoot then, and didn't know much ;   and for that matter, Tom Carton, a regular professional

bronco-buster, was killed that same year by another unbroken mare out of the very same bronco herd, which jumped and kicked sideways at him in an exactly similar manner, only in his case the death-dealing hoof had caught him in the lower part of the body.

What made my injury much worse was that not only did the kick break off a piece of the bone, but it also broke open the cuts so recently healed that had been inflicted by the teeth of the mowing-machine. And it was the same infernal mare that now had done me in again. You may say it was my fault both times, but it did make me hate her like poison.

I had left my rifle at the cabin when I went in to get the mare, but I still had my pistol with me.

Well, this wretch of mine jumped right over me as I fell prostrate, and thinking she was going to trample me to death where I lay helpless I pulled my pistol and fired a shot close to her ears to make her keep off. I was half-minded to kill her, I was so angry, but really if it hadn't been that I was faint with pain I could have laughed to see her pitch and buck until she got rid of that saddle, for as I had undone the latigo strap in order to tighten the cinch, every jump she made shook it looser and looser. Finally she bucked herself clear, and ran off to the spring by the cabin, leaving the saddle still tied to the carcass lying close to where I lay.

I was in a desperate fix. Not only was my leg broken, but the reopened wounds from the mowing-

machine were bleeding freely. I started to try to crawl towards the cabin and fainted. How long I lay there I do not know, but when I recovered consciousness the sun was still high in the sky. I raised myself on my elbows and looked round. It was not a pleasant sight that met my eyes. The wolves and crows had arrived. Hop, hop, hop came a great black crow quite near me. The yellowish grey forms of a dozen coyotes sneaked round a little farther off. In a sudden fury I blazed away at them with four out of the remaining five shots in my pistol. I kept the sixth. Suppose the Cheyennes should happen to come along, I did not propose to be taken alive.

At the shots, the wolves ran off and the crows flapped heavily away. But as they saw I didn't move, the wolves and crows soon came back again. They smelt the blood on me, and their unerring instinct told them that for them it was only a matter of time. They could wait.

That was a long day for me. Lew quite possibly might not come down for another week ; still, there was just the off-chance of it. And hour after hour I lay there and watched the sun sinking towards Pike's Peak, while the wolves lay down and yawned and licked their chops, and the crows croaked their impatience as they walked to and fro. Night would soon fall, and then——!

Suddenly, when the sun was now but a hand's breadth high over the Peak, I saw a black spot on the prairie two or three miles away in the direction of the Divide. It was, it must be, the waggon.

Inch by inch, as it seemed, it drew nearer, and just before sundown it reached the cabin. I could just see the two men alight from it, but of course, stretched flat on the ground as I was, they would not observe me. I shouted at the top of my voice. They took no notice. They did not hear. It was too far. I shouted again. I shouted twenty times over at the very pitch of my voice, and still no notice. A chill wind blew from them to me, and partly stopped the sound. My heart sank. It is dreadful to have the cup actually snatched from your lips. Was I not to be rescued after all? The sun touched the horizon and sank behind it. At that moment the wind fell and there came a calm. I raised myself on my elbows and let out one last, long, despairing hallo. If that failed——!

And then I saw my partner jump out from the cabin, rifle in hand, followed by the other man, and both started running in my direction. I knew then that I was saved.

"Well, what you bin' and done to yourself now?" asked Lew, as he got close.

"Molly's broke my leg," I answered. "I wanted to make her drag in an antelope."

"Well, of all the G——d d——d clumsy . . ." broke out my partner.

He was not sympathetic, but no doubt it was trying to have another interruption to the work of starting the ranch. However, there was no help for it, so he and Jud fixed up a sort of stretcher and carried me in, and tied up my leg with rough skill. Next morning they fixed me a bed in the

waggon, and Jud drove me in to Denver, and once more Dr. Justice mended up my leg for me. There was one thing sure : the worms had not yet eaten those scars left by his previous reconstruction of the leg, neither had the wolves and crows

CHAPTER XII

ON MY OWN

DOCTOR JUSTICE was of course a regular professional man; I should never have dreamed of having any other. But there were others; and to Denver just at this time there had come a man who was a most soul-stirring preacher, and also a most astonishing wonder-worker. I cannot remember the name of the religious denomination that he belonged to, or claimed to belong to, but his miracles were in all men's mouths. He preached that if you would only believe and be converted and let him baptize you properly by immersion in the big ditch from the South Platte which supplied water to Denver you could be cured of any mortal thing. Myself, I never heard him preach; that wasn't my style; but Suse Howell did. Dr. Justice had told me that her terrible epilepsy was incurable, hopelessly incurable. But she listened to that preacher, and she believed, or at any rate thought she'd give him a try.

The consequence was that one day I found myself a member of a small Denver crowd on one side of the Platte ditch, in the middle of which stood the preacher nearly waist-deep in water, while on the

other side there descended from buggies or covered waggons convert after convert, clad in a sort of bathing costume, and they one by one went down into the water and were there put completely under by the preacher and came out again relieved of all their sins. The crowd amid which I stood was unbelieving and not disinclined to scoff.

Down to the water came a man in thin bathing clothes who before conversion had been a notorious bad character. The preacher held up his hands to heaven and prayed fervently and put him under.

" Sock him under again, parson," sang out a scoffer beside me. " Give it to him well. He's the worst man in Denver and he needs it bad."

But the one immersion was reckoned sufficient, and the worst man in Denver crawled out dripping, and so back to his buggy.

Such scoffs, however, were the exception, not the rule ; on the whole the crowd behaved very decently, and when Suse Howell, for instance, went down into the water and was totally immersed you couldn't have heard a murmur.

But the odd thing was that this miracle-working performance, or whatever it was called, did do some at least of the good that was claimed for it. I don't know if it did actually regenerate the worst man in Denver, but Suse Howell's epileptic fits stopped. At least she didn't have any more of them while I was there in Denver, where I stayed on till Lew came in to fetch me out to the ranch.

The ranch had got on splendidly ; Lew had hired a good man to help him and Jud, and he

had also got some freighting teamsters to haul the logs and posts down from the Divide for him. Now the barns, corrals and house were all ready, and things looked really shipshape. But all this work had cost money, and I hadn't brought quite enough out with me from Denver.

By this time, however, we had another city much nearer to us than Denver ; this was Colorado Springs on the Fountain River about twenty-five miles west of our ranch : the new city was built outside the mountains, not very far from the wonderful spring I had seen on my first journey, and it was a very high-toned sort of new town indeed, quite unlike Evans. It was run by a very tony Company, on teetotal lines, and any man there who wanted a drink had to go a couple of miles round the end of the mesa to Colorado City, or Old Town as it was called, where he could find a saloon. So Lew and I drove in to the Springs, as the new town was generally called for short, and we got what coffee and bacon and things we needed for the ranch at the stores there, very good stores they were too. And then I spotted the sign of a bank, a brand new bank, Young's Bank was the name they put up. I hadn't brought along any introductions, but it suddenly struck me that maybe I could draw here on London in the way I regularly did in Denver. I suggested this at once to Lew.

" Wal', mebbe you might," he replied. " But I'd hardly have thought it. You ain't known here."

However, I felt gay, and guessed I could have a try anyway. It wasn't that I had anything

to drink, for you couldn't get such a thing there, and we hadn't been over to Old Town. But I pulled my very rough ranch clothes as tidy as I could and boldly walked right in. There behind the bank counter stood a very fine handsome young fellow, Hayward I learned later his name was, who looked at me interrogatively.

" Anything I can do for you ? "

" Yes," I answered in my most honeyed English tones, " I'd like to draw for thirty pounds on Cox and Co., of London."

He stared. It was a bit abrupt. But my accent reassured him. Lots of Englishmen were concerned in the Company and Dr. W. A. Bell of England was, I think, its chief secretary or manager or something very important in it.

I explained that I had just come in from the ranch on Squirrel Creek ; that hitherto I had been banking in Denver, sixty-five miles off, and thought the Springs, being only twenty-five miles, would be much more convenient. Finally he took me in to speak to Mr. Young, the cashier, which is the same as bank manager in England, and the upshot was that my draft on Cox and Co. for £30 was accepted and I got over $200 in greenbacks. Exchange was about 160 in those days. Out I came triumphant.

" And do you suppose that son of a biscuit would have let me have that money ? " said Lew indignantly when I proudly showed it to him. " He'd more likely have told me to go to Hades ! "

" Well," said I, " he'd have spotted you for an American at once and known you weren't likely to be

drawing on Cox and Co. of London. For me, with my best English accent on, it was probable enough."

But Lew's reply, I regret to say, was quite unprintable.

Ultimately, to the best of my recollection, Young's was merged in a National Bank, and I did business with him for years.

The next thing Lew and I wanted, now the ranch was ready, was a good bunch of cattle : the American stock we had bought of Major Oakes were only a nucleus. We heard of the Berry and Davis lot being for sale. They were Spanish stock and so ought to cost only about half the price of American cattle. A good American steer was quite half as heavy again as a Texas steer and matured a full year earlier. But by using pure American bulls your half-breed steers were as good as American. This Berry and Davis herd was being held somewhere off, I fancy, down the Fountain River. We went after them and came to the conclusion that they would suit us exactly. It was a herd of the longhorned Spanish cattle which Berry and Davis had picked up in New Mexico, and of course they were the same breed as the Texas stock, but these were not so wild ; indeed, many of the cows had been milked by the women in New Mexico. It ended in our buying the lot and taking them to the ranch. Lew had hired a big California Mexican, California Joe he was known as, who helped us most effectively with them. He was an A1 cowman, and could both ride and lasso splendidly, and having our excellent corrals it did not

take long to get them all branded TH on the left hip, which was the brand we had registered. We got some young American bulls to improve the stock and turned them all loose on the range with the lot we had already. How splendid the grazing was in those days when we hadn't another herd within a dozen miles of us. But more were coming. Randall and Crow built a cabin and took up a claim only three miles west of us and proposed to bring a thousand or fifteen hundred of Texas cattle on to the range and other claims also were staked out. We couldn't have it for ever all to ourselves.

And now the final thing was for Lew to bring his family out from Denver, and this he did; he brought his mother and his sister and all their belongings with them. The six-roomed log-house was none too big for so many, but I did get a room to myself in it. That simply had to be.

I think I had better pass as lightly as possible over the events of the next year or so. With Lew I was ever the best of friends, but in truth his family were difficult to live with. Poor Suse was not really cured by her baptismal immersion in the Platte ditch. The fits stopped for a time, and then they came back again as bad as, or even worse than, ever. When she was all right, she was pleasant enough, and she was always most kind to me, but every few weeks these horrible fits recurred and for whole days together she became practically insane: she used to say the most cruel and odious things to everybody in the house, even to her mother. And once when I was out herding

she must have got into my room and carried off my revolver which I had not taken along. Of course I missed it when I got back, and having a shrewd guess as to the trouble I told Lew about it. He cautioned me not to say a word, and made a careful search. Ultimately he recovered it and returned it again to me, warning me never to leave it in my room again but always to keep it with me. A lunatic, for such poor Suse was when the period of the fits was on, when armed with a Colt's navy pistol is a most uncommonly dangerous person to have about the house. After this I moved my bed down to the old cabin alongside the spring, and for the future I slept there, merely coming up to the house for meals.

Of course I was away from the ranch a good deal after the cattle. The whole lot of them drifted down to the Arkansas before the northern blizzards of the next winter, and Jud and I had to go after them and hunt them up on the Spring round-ups. But after all the ranch was my home, and a home with a lunatic at large in it is not exactly pleasant. The upshot of all this was that I made up my mind to buy out Lew's interest ; by the terms of our agreement the partnership was to last two years longer, but I wanted badly to have the ranch to myself. I felt quite an experienced old hand by this time, and boldly imagined myself perfectly able to run a ranch on my own. The negotiations took some time, but ended in my making my bargain. I paid Lew over a good round sum, and he removed his family and himself to the mountains

where he engaged in some business, at this moment
I forget precisely what. Right glad I was to find
myself free of them and absolutely independent
once more. This was in 1873. I hired Tom Russell,
a big Texas cowboy, to be my herder. Tom had
come up from Texas as a hand with a herd of cattle.
Lately he and his Mexican partner, Leonardo Garcia,
generally known as Gus, who hailed from old Mexico,
had been herders looking after the cattle of Randall
and Crow which had been brought in and turned
loose on our range, and I had got to know both
of them pretty well. Tom was an A1 cowboy
and had various things to recommend him. When
he left Randall and came to herd for me his friend
Gus stayed on with Randall, and as Randall's
place was only three miles off from mine it followed
that we saw a good deal of each other. Tom and
Gus had a few cattle of their own, which ran on
the range : it was in cattle that they were partners.
Tom was well known in the cow-camps and had
rather a curious reputation : it was understood
that he had killed a man down in Texas in a rough-
and-tumble fight, killed him justifiably. Tom
never posed as a desperado ; never did he talk of
the killing ; but the idea of it was always there,
and men looked upon him as slightly alarming.
Moreover, the idea of that killing remained in his
own mind, for though, as I said, he never talked
of it, yet in his dreams the memory of it would
come back, and he lived the episode over again,
gritting his teeth, and breathing hard, and clutching
with fierce fingers for his enemy's throat. It

will be simplest if I tell here a little story of him
at my ranch; the thing happened a trifle later
on that same year. Cattlemen prided themselves
on being extremely hospitable to each other, and
if in hard weather a party turned up at a ranch
without their blankets the cowmen there would
take them into their beds rather than compel them
to lie coverless on the floor. Such a party turned
up one night at my ranch when already there were
some others staying with me who had brought their
bedding along. Result, each man of those who
were provided took in one of the unprovided ones,
and they all doubled up like this. Tom Russell
had thus taken into his blankets a stranger, who
knew him well enough by name anyway and how
he was said to have killed his man down in Texas.

I had the door open from my room into that
where Tom and the rest were sleeping. In the
night we were all startled awake by an appealing
voice, " Mr. Russell, I ain't done nuthin'. Mr.
Russell, I'll apologize. Mr. Russell, whatever it
is, I beg your pardon." And at the same time we
could also hear Tom gritting his teeth, and breathing
hard, and reaching for his bedfellow's throat. We
did manage to get Tom waked at last, and we
explained things to the unlucky gentleman who
had been doubled up with him, telling him that
it was not his heart's blood Tom was after but
that of his dream enemy down there in Texas.
Yes, Tom Russell was certainly looked on as a rather
formidable man to tackle. And perhaps I was not
altogether sorry to have him on that account either.

CHAPTER XIII

THE BATTLE OF THE BULLS

"CAPTAIN," said Gus to me, "you hear that bull?" We listened. From far off across the rolling swells of the prairie came a voice like the shrill blare of a war trumpet. It was the full-throated challenge of a mighty bull.

"That got to be Mr. Randall's big red bull," said Gus. "I know the way he talk. He the boss bull of Brackett Creek; and them Brackett Creek cattle coming right now down the gulch t'other side that hill yonder."

It was a glorious July day and the three of us, Gus and I and Tom Russell, were riding along the slopes that stretch downwards from Holcombe Hollow, driving before us all the cattle we could find to the round-up near Big Springs, eight miles east of me. Fred Pracht had taken up a claim there and brought in a small herd of Texas cattle. Also Nusbaum Brothers had started a ranch with well over a thousand head north-west of me, so that the range was getting to be pretty full.

At the sound of that shrill challenge a mile away every pair of horns was lifted up in the band of cows and young steers in front of us, and every head was turned expectantly in that direction,

while several of the beasts lowed in a subdued hesitating fashion in answer. But there was another answer also given to the challenge, and of a different quality. In the very rear of our bunch marched sedately the big white bull to whom the cowboys of the range had given the name of General Grant. He was the boss of Holcombe Hollow, and no other bull there durst dispute his rights. " Let us have peace ! " he always seemed to say (like his great namesake), and if any other bull offered to argue with him on the matter, the General, in the interests of peace, knocked him endways in a minute. He was a noble brute to see. His glossy hide shone like white satin in the sun ; on his broad brow and between his horns was a frontlet of crisp-curled hair, and from his massive neck and chest a dewlap hung down that almost swept the ground.

Now, when his rival's challenge rang on the air, he roused him from his leisurely dignity in the rear, and trotted eagerly to the front. And as he went he raised his head, and from his deep throat he blew a shattering blast of sound that set the air a-quiver, a blast full of defiance and of pride. Like the Mexican, he had recognized in that challenge the voice of a foeman worthy of his steel, and this was his answer.

" It 'minds me of the cavalry bugles before a charge," said Tom, while all our ears were still ringing with the blast.

Tom knew what fighting was ; he had seen four years' service when North and South tried the dread arbitrament of war.

"In my country," observed the Mexican, "often we have the *fiesta de toros*, but sometimes when the bull come into the plaza he seem as if he don't care to fight. Then the soldiers sound the trumpets at him, and that makes any bull fighting mad right off." Strange that the trumpet-call should rouse the fierce masculine fighting instinct in man and brute alike !

Again, from beyond the hill there came the defiance of the Brackett Creek champion, and again the great white bull lifted up his mighty voice and blared his fierce reply. And, as with head thrown back, he spoke, the sight revived for me the recollection of the pose of the stag in Landseer's picture of "The Challenge."

But now, in the hearts of the young steers, these trumpet-calls awoke uncertain, half-conceived desires ; they tossed their heads, and leaped in the air, and gave short bellows, like weak echoes of the fanfares of the master-bulls. They squared up to one another, half in earnest, and clashed their slender horns together, and dealt each other mimic thrusts and blows, as if to say, "That's how they do it ; and there's a rib-roaster for you." So you may see a parcel of small boys spar at each other and dance about in ecstasy when a fight between two big fellows is imminent.

"Them cattle thieves on the frontier between Mexico and Texas," said Tom, "allus has to shoot the boss bulls first if they want to run off a herd quietly. The smaller ones don't have so much to say, but the rumpus which these tonguey old

warriors make when they meet another herd and begin to look for trouble is enough to give away the whole show."

As he spoke, from round the corner of the hill, out on to the plain of tawny sun-cured grass there streamed into our sight a moving mass of many-coloured animals, red and white, and black, and roan. They were the Brackett Creek cattle, and a scant quarter of a mile now separated them from us. We reined in our sweating ponies, and stood at gaze to watch the meeting. No sooner had the two herds sighted one another than a chorus of lowing of cows and steers and bleating of calves burst forth on both sides ; cries of greeting these, and not of hostility. But a great red bull with a white face detached himself from the strangers and trotted heavily forward in our direction.

" You were right, Gus," said Tom to the Mexican, " that's him ; that's Brigham Young, old Randall's boss bull." It was considered on the range a first-class joke to name a master bull after the Mormon Prophet of polygamy.

The Holcombe Hollow champion was ready for his foe, and stood on guard fifty yards in front of his own herd, pawing the ground with either fore-foot alternately. His hoofs tossed the sand in showers twenty feet aloft to rain down again on his broad back and snowy sides. He bowed his huge neck into an arch, and put his mouth to the ground and roared staccato thunders that seemed to make the solid earth tremble beneath us.

" Hark to him," said Tom. " He's a-telling

old Brigham ' Come on, till I wipe up the ground with you! Come on, I can whip you the best day you ever saw! Come on, you ain't no bull. I've got yearlings in Holcombe Hollow could walk over you."

The red bull came up to within thirty yards of the white, and there he paused ; he, too, pawed sand into the air with his hoofs, and bowed his mighty neck and roared a fresh defiance, mouthing it against the ground, that seemed to smoke with the fierce hot breath of his nostrils.

" Now he's a-talking back," said Tom. " Come over here, you coward," says he, " come and see me knock you crazy. You dursn't step a yard this way. Go home and fight your yearlings, and don't come anigh me ! "

The General felt the taunts. Down on his knees he went, and ploughed the earth up with his horns, and screamed out a high, shrill, jubilant Tarantara-ra-ra. Then he sprang up, the very image of savage fury. Huge brute as he was he leaped high in the air, all four feet off the ground, and made a rush towards his foe. I looked to see him charge headlong down upon him ; but no, he stopped again, and began to paw dirt once more.

Now scarce ten yards separated them, and each gathered himself for the shock. Closer and closer yet they drew, the feet well under the body, neck, back, and shoulders forming one great arch, each champion the very embodiment of bovine strength up for the fray. They were both silent now, saving their breath for the struggle. Foot by foot and

inch by inch they closed, each with the glowing red eye bent warily upon the foe, as, stiff and tense, they circled round each other almost at arm's length, like boxers waiting for an opening.

Crash! The two heads struck together with a sudden clap that you might have heard a mile away. Broad brow drove hard against brow, horn clashed with horn, as the champions hurled at one another with might and main. They dealt neither blow nor thrust as yet, but forehead to forehead each drove straight forward, with his whole weight, seeking to bear his enemy back; their struggling feet ploughed up the ground; their hard-drawn breaths came in quick pants. They stamped like two wrestlers locked in a desperate grip, with every muscle straining to its very utmost. Hurrah for our champion; the white bull gains ground; inch by inch the red is being borne back. But the namesake of the prophet is not beaten yet. Now is the time, now or never! He gathers all his forces for one supreme effort, humps his huge shoulders high, and with one desperate heave he bears the General back a yard or more. The sweat of battle stains our champion's glossy sides with dark streaks and patches; his breath comes in short, quick pants; but he is not done yet He, too, collects all his force in turn, and with irresistible assaults he bears the struggling, reluctant, breathless Brigham back, back the full stretch of the yard he had gained, and another, and another yet, and then two more to boot. The panting red bull reels in the effort to keep his feet; he

must either turn or be overthrown. With a sudden twist of the neck he disengages his forehead from his foe's, and springs sideways to save himself from falling. The General hurls himself on his enemy, his brandished horns raking the exposed side and flank of the other. No courage is of any avail when thus taken in flank and rear, and the great red bull has nothing for it but to run. Hard upon his heels follows the white, thrusting him in flank and quarter with cruel lunges of the horn. But the hide is thick and tough, and the horn points lack sharpness ; the hair may fly in tufts and great long welts be scored along the skin, but the horn is never driven home, and the red bull, galloping hard, escapes at last beyond the reach of his conqueror. To use the language of the ring, it was the end of round one.

" Them bulls go on till sundown if we don't stop 'em," said Gus, as he watched the two warriors, now some thirty yards apart, face each other once more, and paw the earth with angry feet, and with labouring breath begin to roar fresh defiance and hoarse invitation to renew the fray.

It was clear that as soon as they had recovered their strength the battle would be joined again, even more fiercely than before. They stood like two armies facing each other after a fiercely fought but indecisive struggle, exhausted for the moment but savagely determined to try conclusions again.

" Like enough, these two bulls never would have fought if we hadn't druv 'em together," said Tom, philosophically. " Both of 'em was satisfied with

being boss at home. But now they've met they can't be content without fighting it to a finish, and Brigham would sure outlast the General. You bet he's the boss bull anywheres around here and no error."

"Come along," said I; "business is business. We must shove the herds on to the round-up. Our day's work is still before us, and if we hustle 'em round a bit lively, these two warriors will get a chance to forget their quarrel. It's strange, though, how keen they are to go on fighting once they've begun. They've got their blood up and they'd rather fight now than drink or eat or sleep, or do anything else. It's just the natural animal instinct in brutes, I suppose."

"There's men like that, too, I've seen," said Tom Russell.

So he had, and the dead man down there in Texas was one of them.

CHAPTER XIV

A TEXAS NURSERY

ON a blazing hot noon in early summer I was riding around over the range looking for a stray horse. The endless rolling surface of the prairie seemed absolutely bare of cattle, so far, at least, as one could depend upon what the eye told one. For it was one of the days when the " smoke " was strong, " smoke " being the name we used to give to the mirage. Out in Colorado all the baffling uncertainty of vision that makes for mystery, all illusion, all glamour, belong to the dazzling hours of midday and not to the gloaming.

In the early morning, and towards evening, there is no " smoke " and no mystery, for out there on the great plains, five thousand feet above sea level in the very driest part of the American continent, the air is of an incredible transparency. Forty miles from my ranch the huge red granite dome of Pike's Peak heaved up its beetling crags against the western sky, and at sunrise every crack and crevice of the rocks showed as sharp and clear-cut as though they were only half a mile off. Northwards the stem of one solitary pine, ten miles away, made a thin black line against the sky, and I once

knew a single horseman detected by the keen sight of a frontiers-man standing in front of my ranch over on Holcombe bluffs across a distance of fully two leagues.

But as the summer sun mounted high and poured his scorching rays on the bare ground there came a change. The lowest layer of air absorbed the heat from the heated soil and presently began to rise up in wavering currents such as one may observe to quiver perpetually over the mouth of a furnace.

Through this flickering veil of mirage all things were seen distorted, shifting, uncertain. A solitary soapweed a hundred yards away might suddenly stand up and develop legs and become a horse; again the horse's back would swell and arch itself into a great hump, and lo! there stood a buffalo instead; presto! the buffalo would sink, elongate himself, and be transformed into a thicket of reeds, shaking in the wind, alongside a pool of clear delicious water. And then in a moment the scene would change back again, the illusion pass, and the common soapweed was a weed once more.

However, I had no time to waste over fancies, but pushed on in search of my stray horse, on whom, if chance willed, and the " smoke " were not too confusing, I might happen at any minute. And at last I thought I had him when I made out a large animal by itself some way off upon a hill.

" It can't be a cow," said I to myself, " for the cattle have all left the high prairie and the sand-hills. This heat has sent them into the water below the ranch to drink."

I rode nearer. Was it really my stray? I fancied so. And then I heard a sound that undeceived me. It was not a horse at all, but a cow, lowing most mournfully, and looking ever anxiously back over the prairie. That unhappy voice told plainly enough that she was in dire distress over her calf, and I galloped up to see what was wrong. She was a big white American cow, one of the bunch Lew and I bought from Major Oakes; she had a strain of shorthorn blood in her veins, and there, sure enough, about three hundred yards behind her, lay her newly-born calf, under the scanty shadow of a soapweed. She had been brought out from the States, and came of gentle domestic stock, too domestic, perhaps, for life on the range.

The calf was not yet strong enough to follow its mother over the three long miles to the watering place, where all the rest had gone; and when his strength gave out he had lain down in the only bit of shade he could find. His mother, tortured by thirst, had hurried on without him, and then halted, with divided mind. Thirst pulled her feverishly on towards the water: mother-love plucked at her heart-strings to drag her back to her calf. And here the poor fool had stood for an hour, making the prairie echo to her distracted wails, and telling any wolf, lurking within a mile of her, that the bell was ringing for his dinner. The first spring Lew and I had the Oakes cattle there the buffalo wolves killed three or four young cows with their calves like that.

I dismounted beside the calf, picked him up,

heaved him into the saddle, and climbed back and settled myself there with him in my lap.

Small chance should I have had of doing it, if the mother had been one of my war-like Texas cows, a fierce, wild daughter of the desert. But this gentle, idiotic creature offered no objection ; she was accustomed to devolving her maternal responsibilities on man, and she shambled along behind me with docile content, only lowing at intervals to tell her son she was there, as we made straight for the water-holes.

There I left the pair, safe in the protection of numbers, for there were a thousand head of range cattle strung all up and down the creek.

I turned back to the rolling prairie, where I was still hoping to find my stray horse, and as I went I noticed half a dozen dun and brindle Texas cows, who had already slaked their thirst, travelling steadily away from the water in the same direction as myself. A few young heifers and steers accompanied them, though the mass of the cattle, as I well knew, would stay by the water till the heat of the day was over ; but this party of long-horned, long-legged Texas ladies clearly had business elsewhere. They struck into one of the innumerable cattle trails leading from the high pastures to the water and pressed up it, travelling one close behind the other at a steady walk that occasionally became a trot. I rode parallel to them, curious to see the goal they were making for so eagerly.

Up we went into the high rolling sand-hills, and there, in the middle of them, in a little cup-like

hollow, I saw a regular Texas nursery. Eight little dun-coloured Texas calves lay there, squatted close to the sandy ground with which their coats matched so well, their heads lying out flat, with the chins pressed down on the sand, just as little antelope fawns would have crouched. In this pose they were all but invisible. Beside them lay two elderly Texas cows, whose office had been to guard the crèche.

The mothers, who had travelled till now in perfect silence, began to low loudly and lovingly when they caught sight of their offspring, and in a moment each young hopeful had jumped up and rushed to his own dam, where his wriggling tail and nuzzling head, the busy lips frothing with milk, soon showed he was getting the dinner he had waited for so patiently. Meantime the two guardian cows had risen to their feet, and lost no time in starting off in their turn to make their trip to the water, leaving their own two calves safe in the care of the rest of the band.

The system of mutual protection was perfect. Brer' Wolf might prowl around and watch with hungry eyes till his lips watered—there was no chance for him to get veal for his dinner while the sharp horns of those fierce Texas mothers guarded their children. Broadly speaking, one might say the Texas cow, the cow of the wilderness, had evolved an institution that has enabled her and her offspring to survive the dangers of savage life.

This institution has been long superseded by

the civilized life of the farm for the well-bred short-horn cow ; but take her away from her sheltered surroundings and turn her loose on the range, and she is as helpless as most duchesses would be if left on a desert island. The pedigree daughter of fifty prize-winners must inevitably succumb to the dangers of her new life unless she has initiative enough to revert to the social system of her own primitive ancestors who fought with the wolf and bear in the woodlands of early Britain.

I left my little garrison of Texas cows to hold the fort, and as I turned back to the water-holes the first thing I espied was Tom Russell mounted on the stray. He rode up, and told how he had found and followed up the trail of the wanderer, a new purchase, not yet wonted to the bell-mare, and how he had roped him and shifted his saddle on to him, leaving his own horse loose to find his way to the caballada, as the Mexicans call a band of horses, knowing that the tribal instinct of the range horse would take him straight back to join his companions.

I showed Tom the American cow and calf, safe now amid the crowd along the creek, and told him of the Texas nursery I had seen in the sand-hills.

"I know that band right enough," said he. "Thar's an old brindle cow with rings out to the ends of her horns that leads 'em. Likely she's the mother of most of 'em too. She's old enough, sure ; old enough to vote, almost."

Add two to the number of rings you can distinctly

count on a cow's horns and you will get her age.

" Well," said I, " if she's the mother, that would explain some things. Those cows were as like as so many peas. So are the calves."

The calves were Texas bred. Next year's crop would be half-blood American. Texas bulls were taboo in Colorado and liable to be shot at sight. We wanted to improve on them.

" That's how it is with most of these bands," he returned, looking down along the creek, which was fairly alive with cattle, some drinking, some wallowing in the pools; others were rubbing their heads and necks where they could find a good place, using the rough clay edges of the banks as a sub- stitute for a scratching-post. Young steers were having mock combats with one another or butting at the heifers. And over all rang the shrill blare of the challenges of the bulls. " They're mixed up some now," he continued, " but you know how when they go off to feed towards night they'll string out twenty and thirty in a band. These bands are mostly of one blood. A cow's heifer calves like to stay with her after they're weaned, and in a year or two they're having more calves of their own, and the whole lot stick by one another. That's how it comes that the cows in a band favour each other so much, and if you spot one of 'em anywheres around you can bet that bar accidents the rest ain't far off."

" In fact, the mothers are the basis on which cow society is organized," I said. " Sounds like what the scientific men call matriarchy. That

only means a system in which descent is traced through the mother, and the children all belong to her tribe. I was thinking something like that coming here after watching the Texas nursery."

" Well, that's about how it works out on the range," said the cowboy. " You can't keep no herd-book pedigrees of this wild stock. There's twenty bulls here, and they range all over the place, going with this band to-day and with t'other to-morrow, as may chance. They ain't got no family ties. Hark to 'em now ! Oh, yes, they can all talk mighty loud, but old Brigham's the boss of the lot."

From far down the creek challenge after challenge rang out, as bull after bull called to his rivals that he had found his chosen mate.

Ta-ran-ta-ra-ra-ra they went, like the stirring bugle calls that summon men to arms. To right, to left, on the hill and by the water, came those harsh, defiant cries, shattering the air, as each one proudly announced, " She's here, she's mine. Come one, come all ; here stand I in my rights as a bull. Beware." Yet in spite of all this loud talk there were not as many fights as one might have expected. For one thing, the bulls were, comparatively speaking, so few. Nine-tenths of the bull calves were destined by man's intervention to be turned into beef-steers, or else to bow their necks to the yoke and become work-oxen, and in consequence the competition among the remainder was far less fierce than it would have been under natural conditions.

And then the bulls had had their trials of strength at the beginning of the season and each knew just whom he could beat and who was his master, as boys at school knew in the days when every boy was expected to use his fists as a matter of course. So the boss bull of the range, the same big, red, broad-horned warrior with a white face that betokened some Hereford blood, trotted up and down the creek as usual, trumpeting defiance everywhere and visiting each band in turn till he settled down with his accepted mate for the day, and his envious rivals betook themselves elsewhere.

" Ole Brigham goes jes' whar' he likes, and he makes 'em all stand round," said the cowboy, as we sat on our ponies watching them. " They dursn't none of 'em tackle him, an' he knows it. Look at him now, standing guard over that black cow he's took up with. No other bull can come within fifty yards of her."

Not a single rival on the range had a chance with Brigham, and combinations of two against one were not allowed. The etiquette of the range prescribes that when two bulls fight no other shall interfere, and the duel is fairly fought out between the pair. But on this occasion a new element presented itself.

" Hello ! " cried Tom, " here's a variety show. Here come them ten young bulls from Sam Hertzel's that old Randall has jest bought and turned loose. They're not common range bulls at all, but reg'lar high-toned pedigree stock, and I'm curious to see how they'll shape."

Over the hill came ten two-year-old roan short-horns, as like one another as ten peas. They had just been introduced on the scene by Mr. Randall, who had a judicious desire to improve the quality of our common stock which ran indiscriminately all over the Squirrel Creek gulches. He had gone to Sam Hertzel's, on Chico, and procured these valuable animals from that thrifty Dutchman, who kept a good herd of well-bred dairy cows, and had bought a magnificent pedigree shorthorn bull, the first ever seen in Colorado, for $1,000. Sam kept his prize bull in a stable, and on his ranch there was a great pasture fenced in for his young animals, while during the summer he took care to see his breeding stock close-herded by day and corralled at night, so as to keep the breed pure. Consequently these ten youngsters had spent an untroubled youth of peaceful brotherhood, and were good friends together.

But when at the sight of the ten new-comers Brigham's loud challenge burst upon the air, the novel sound woke the ancestral instinct of fight in them at once, and they ran eagerly forward to begin their new life. With the unhesitating courage of ignorance the liveliest among them put down his head and charged straight at Brigham, who was going through all the orthodox prelimin-aries to the combat, fiercely pawing the ground and making the dirt fly with his forefeet. The shock of the two-year-old's charge was a trifle to the scarred winner of a hundred fights, and with one contemptuous shove he pushed him aside and

sent him spinning twenty feet away. But then came an episode that was quite irregular. The other nine were ignorant of the etiquette of the range. They should have stood still and looked on, or taken it in turn to come up and be knocked down one by one.

They did nothing of the kind. They all ran at Brigham in a mass and waded in with the enthusiasm of ignorance. They pounded that astonished sultan of the range in the ribs, and they prodded him in the stern; they hit him on both sides at once and at either end; they punched him hard in the flanks and knocked the breath out of his huge body, until poor Brigham was in sad case. He had never been so beset before, and in five minutes he was the most demoralized bull out, and found himself puffing and blowing a hundred yards away from his chosen stamping-ground.

He was an ex-champion who had been knocked out, while these ten impudent young rascals from Chico were shrilling pæans of victory at the pitch of their youthful voices, and rioting and frisking round in the most unseemly manner. Tom Russell nearly fell off his horse with laughing.

" Serves old Brigham right," said he. " He's been knocking all the others around till he thinks he's king, and now he's learnt a lesson. But these youngsters will all turn to fighting with one another before they're a day older, and then he'll be boss again same as before."

Tom was right as usual; long ere nightfall their unholy alliance, of ten against one, was dissolved,

and the frivolous members of it had distributed themselves around and gone off, some one way and some another, with the various bands where they had found mates for the time being. But the alliance that guarded the Texas nursery remained an indissoluble bond.

CHAPTER XV

HIDE AND SEEK WITH DOG-SOLDIERS

THERE was quite an excitement in the cow-camps when Joe Fallon, who had a small cattle ranch not far from mine, went and got married. That was because of the novelty of the thing. Of course there were a good few married ranchmen up on the Divide, or settled along such creeks as the Fountain, where farming by irrigation was carried on, but among the pioneer cattle-men out on the Great Plains in the early seventies I do not remember a single one who had a wife. So when a muslin curtain was seen draping the window of Joe's cabin, sure sign of a woman having taken up her abode there, we bachelors of the cow-camps hesitated a little before intruding on the newly-made bride. Pretty soon, however, Joe turned up one morning at my ranch, and confided to me a secret. Mrs. Joe was discontented. I don't mean discontented with him of course, for even if it were so Joe wasn't exactly the sort of man to proclaim it ; she was discontented with the grub. She was tired of living on beans and bacon, and Joe had nothing else for her. She had expressed a longing for fresh meat, but the weather was too hot to kill a beef. There were plenty of

antelope running around indeed, but Joe had knocked the front sight of his rifle all awry somehow, and no man alive can kill antelope on the plains with a rifle that doesn't shoot straight. So here was Joe come to ask if I would lend him my Sharpe's ·50 calibre in order that he might kill an antelope for his pining bride.

Lend it! Of course I would. Who could be such a brute as to say no, when the wife of a cattleman longed for savoury venison? Besides, I was just off with Judge Randall's outfit to take a herd of beeves to The Springs, and I didn't want it anyhow. There would certainly be nothing to shoot along the road, and as for wanting it in The Springs, why Colorado Springs was the most quiet, orderly little town in those days you ever saw, at least for anyone who didn't deliberately run his head into mischief. Naturally, if one chose to go round the saloons in Old Town, Colorado City, he might easily come in for a shooting scrape, but then one needn't go there. And thus it happened that Joe Fallon got my precious rifle on loan, not without many injunctions to take the very best care of it.

Also I lent my Colt's pistol to Gus while I made the Springs. He was to go off seventy-five miles south and fetch up a roan bull and some cows and calves of my brand which had wandered off down the Arkansaw, and of which honest Bob Courbet had sent me word. But there were some bad characters down on the lower Arkansaw, and I thought it just as well that Gus should not go unarmed. Consequently, I myself was left with nothing what-

ever in the way of weapons. What was the odds?
The country was quite quiet; there had been no
Indian troubles for nearly three years, and we had
all settled it in our minds that there were never
going to be any again. Colorado was becoming
quite too civilized for that sort of thing.

A week later, having safely delivered the beeves,
I was sitting in the grand-stand at the fair in Colorado
Springs, looking on at the trotting races, when
I felt a tap on my shoulder, and turning I beheld
Fred Pracht, a Dutchman, and a right good fellow,
whose ranch lay about ten miles from mine.

"Have you heard the news?" he asked me
quietly.

"No," said I, "what's up? Has the Colorado
City marshal shot another of the boys this time?"

"Worse than that," said Fred. "The Dog-
soldiers are loose; those infernal Cheyenne Indians
have left their reservation and are raising Cain
all along the Arkansaw."

"Sure?" I cried.

"Sure," said he. "Dan Holden's raised a party
of a hundred men and is following 'em up. But I
doubt they'll run off every loose horse on the southern
ranches."

"Great Scott!" said I. "My horses!" I stood
aghast. My ranch was south of the Divide, on
the Arkansaw slope, and my band of horses with
the bell-mare were running loose in the hills about
the head of Big Sandy. Every penny I could
spare that year I had been putting into horse
stock, and I had just bought from a Texas outfit

a couple of the prettiest cow-ponies any man wants to see, and above all, there was my pet saddle horse, Black Tom, who could race a bit if he was wanted to, for he had in his veins the blood of a grandson of English " Tranby."

What was to be done ? I must try to save them, but how about getting a gun ? In two minutes I had made up my mind, and was on my way to the restaurant where I usually took my grub when I was in The Springs. The news of the Indian outbreak was spreading like wildfire, and the town was roused ; excited ranchmen dashed into stables, flung on their saddles, and dashed out again, clattering headlong down the street regardless of the city ordinance against furious riding. All the bars were crowded with men, and the gunsmiths' shops were jam-full. The Springs was arming itself in haste. I pushed my way through the shouting, pressing throng into the backroom of the restaurant, and seized hold of the proprietor.

" Jimmy," said I, " can you lend me a gun ? There isn't one to be had in this town now for love or money."

" Sure and I will," said he good-naturedly. " I'm not going on the war-path at my time of life, and I don't want it meself. Mrs. Binney, ma'am," and he called to his wife in an inner room, " where's me gun ? Can't ye find it for me ? "

I heard Mrs. Binney rummaging under the bed, and presently she emerged with a very dusty fire-arm ; it was a Warner carbine, an early form of breechloader, rimfire, ·50 calibre. Further search

produced seven big copper cartridges, some of them a good deal bent and bulged.

" That's me gun," said Jimmy proudly ; " sure, didn't I bring ut with me when we crossed the Plains two years ago ? But I've niver fired ut off since."

I threw open the breech, and saw that it was unloaded ; I put my eye to the muzzle to see what the rifling was like, and, behold, all was darkness ; the barrel was choked with rust, dust, and dirt. A cupful of petroleum and a stick, however, soon altered this, and sallying out on the street I ran up against Fred Pracht again.

" Hello !¡" said he, " so you got a gun. Is she a good gun ? "

" Try her if you like," I answered, handing it over to him.

I chose a middling good-looking cartridge out of the precious seven, and he stuffed it into the chamber.

" What'll I shoot at ? " said Fred.

There was a big empty dry-goods case standing on a vacant lot opposite.

" Try a shot at the label on that case over there," I said.

Hardly were the words spoken when the rifle was at his shoulder. Fred was no slouch of a shot —and he pulled the trigger. The hammer fell, but only with a snap ; there was no report ; she had missed fire. He threw open the breech and twisted the cartridge round so as to bring a fresh part of the rim under the striker. Snap, again ; there was a perceptible pause, but this time it

was only a hang-fire, and whang-g-g she went. We ran across to the box, and lo ! the bullet had missed the whole thing at about twenty yards. Fred handed me back the rifle.

" I'd as lief take a good hard wood club to fight Indians with as that thing," was the sarcastic comment.

Sadly I agreed with him, and the rifle was returned to its old quarters under Mrs. Binney's bed.

But go I must anyway, so in the company of Fred and two other ranchmen I set out ; all were well heeled of course, excepting myself, and I had made up my mind to strike straight for Fallon's ranch in order to reclaim my own beloved Sharp's. As we rode southwards across the Divide, alarming reports met us. The red fiends had burned Shuter's mill ; they had run off all Dan Holden's brood mares ; nay, we presently heard that they had cut behind us, making direct for The Springs, and had doubtless sacked and burned it already—no tale was too wild to find credence. On we pushed far into the moonless night ; Fred and I, as it chanced, were riding in front, and the other pair following us. Suddenly something loomed up in the darkness just ahead ; our straining eyes discovered figures leaping to right and left of the trail, and our anxious ears heard the sharp, ominous click-click of rifle hammers drawn to full cock.

" Friends ! " we shouted both together, " we're friends. Don't shoot." " Oh, all right," to us out of the darkness came the answer. " We-uns only thought as how you-uns mout be Injuns."

In the black night we had stumbled up against two hunters, footing it into The Springs behind their horses, which were heavily loaded down with antelope meat to sell. Indians? No, they had seen no Injuns, but they had cut their trail further south. There was two to three hundred of 'em to judge by the pony tracks. Some shod horses there were along too, which showed as how they had stolen a lot of stock from the whites. With a pang I remembered that my two Texas ponies were freshly shod. Forward again we pressed; by noon next day we reached the Southern ranges, and now at last I found myself riding alone; the others struck out for their own ranches, while I kept steadily on steering for Joe Fallon's. Alone indeed! On either hand stretched away the yellow undulations of the great plains, infinite, empty, silent. I might have been alone on earth; nothing met the eye but sun and plain. Stop! what was that? Black forms, travelling in a long line, distorted and vague through the dim flickering mirage. Horsemen? Indians? Yes? No, by George! it's only cattle, after all, stringing out on their way in to water. And now here was Joe Fallon's. I rode up eagerly to the cabin. No smoke was visible.

" Hello, the house ! "

No answer. I got down and looked in. The muslin curtains were still in the window, but the cabin was vacant. Had the Indians got them? It gave me the horrors to think of it. I knew well enough what would be the awful fate of any white woman who should fall alive into their clutches.

Stay; here was a message written on the door, scrawled with the end of a burnt stick, " Gone to Romaine's." Oh, of course. Mrs. Fallon had been one of the Romaine girls, and old Romaine's ranch was off up in the mountains. Joe was a sensible man ; he'd done just as one might have guessed.

The mountain ranch was a safe refuge from the Cheyennes, whose hunting-grounds were the open plains, and who never dared to trespass inside the great barrier of the Rockies. But here was I, unarmed except for a sheath-knife, and my gun was forty miles off at Romaine's. Should I go after it or see to my horses ? The thought of Black Tom carried the day, and I pushed on for my ranch. All was quiet and empty on either side of the track ; and as the sun went down and night fell I watched with intense anxiety for the gleam of a hostile camp fire. None could I detect, but nevertheless the Indians might be anywhere, and I could almost hear my own heart beat in the stillness. Suddenly out of the dark came the shrill nicker of a pony stallion, off somewhere to the east of the trail. He had winded my horse. I was instantly on the alert. None of the ranchmen let their stallions run loose, so the sound was most suspicious. I got off and held my own horse's muzzle, to keep him from answering, and led him away off the trail till we were well out of earshot. Then I got on him again, and making a circle round approached my cabin. I felt for the latch and pulled it up ; all was silent in the house. I struck a match ; everything was undisturbed. I curtained the window with a blanket,

lit a fire, and cooked a hasty meal. Then came the question where I should sleep. I went and stood outside under the stars and considered. The house was visible for half a mile away, and besides that the waggon trail led right to it. If the Indians were near and on the move they were bound to see it, and if I were caught in it with no gun my home would be a death-trap for me. No; the very best place to hide at night is on the bare face of the prairie; all places on the prairies at night are exactly like one another, and no one looking for a fugitive has any more reason to search here than there. The odds are a hundred to one on the fugitive who lies still. In the darkness I could play hide and seek with the Dog-soldiers, and have a very good chance to get the better of them. I took my horse and led him off a mile and lay down on his rope.

I have often read in story books of a man tying the picket rope or even the bridle-rein to his own arm, so that the horse might not get away from him while he slept; but it is a risky thing to do. If a coyote scares the horse and he starts to run, the man tied to him must almost surely be dragged to death. The dodge my partner taught me was to lie down with the rope under you so that the horse cannot pull it away without instantly waking you and giving you a chance to seize it in your hands and stop him. Likely enough he will wake you half a dozen times during the night, but so much the better if there is danger around. Every time I waked that night I listened and peered into the darkness that stood

round me like a wall ; but nothing approached the spot where I lay. If there were any Indians on the prowl, they prowled elsewhere. There was one thought, moreover, that helped me to sleep secure : I knew that every Indian hates to risk getting himself killed at night. He has some very queer ideas of his own about a future life, and he believes that an unlucky brave to whom that happens has to put in his time in the sweet by and by in pitch darkness for ever and ever. It is very curious how useful to us a savage superstition can sometimes be.

At last the morning star was up, and with the earliest twilight I sped towards the hills where my horse herd ran. Soon I made out black objects moving. Was it they ? I counted them—eleven—that was two short of the proper number, and then came the faint tinkle of the mare's bell, and my weary pony pricked up his ears, and whinnied a greeting to his friends. Black Tom was there. The missing two were that last bought pair of Texas ponies. Should I leave the band and hunt for them. No ; it was best to make sure of what I had in my hand, and I shifted my saddle on to Black Tom. Hurrah ! No war pony that was ever foaled could catch me now, and joyfully I whooped up the herd towards the western mountains at a swinging gallop. Every few miles I changed on to a fresh horse, and it was not very long after noon when I had them safe inside the Rockies, and the panting ponies halted at the bars leading into old Romaine's pasture. And here at the door of Romaine's house was a

bright, pretty brunette with sparkling eyes, and my Sharp's rifle in her little hands. " Oh, say, mister, here's your gun. Joe's been mighty anxious about you. He's gone off now into town to inquire after you, for he was feared as you'd be wanting it powerful bad."

And thus it came about that I not only saved my horses, but recovered my gun. How about those strayed Texas ponies ? Alas, the Indians got them, or got one of them anyhow. Lucky, too, it was that they didn't get me. When I came back to look at their tracks next day, I was aghast to discover that it must indeed have been an Indian stallion who nickered when he winded my pony that night as I rode along the trail. I had passed within half a mile of their camp all unconscious of their proximity. It was hide and seek that night with me and the Dog-soldiers, and neither of us found the other. Did I get any compensation for my lost ponies ? Well, it happened that Dan Holden's party of cowboys came in sight of the raiders some fifteen miles east of my place, and Andy Wilson tried a long shot at the devils, and killed a pony. I found the pony lying there still two days later when I went out to hunt for my strays, and sure enough it was one of my missing pair. I fetched the pincers and a clinch-cutter, and stripped the four new shoes off him, and those four shoes, value seventy-five cents, were all the compensation that I ever got from the Dog-soldiers for the theft of my two ponies. But I didn't grumble much. Hadn't I saved Black Tom, to say nothing of my scalp ?

CHAPTER XVI

A BULL IN A BARN

TOM RUSSELL and I got along very well, but he was rather a way-up cowpuncher for so modest-sized a bunch as mine, and after a while he left me to take charge of a far bigger and more important herd. I picked up another cowboy named Kizer who had come up from Texas with a herd, though originally he was a " mean white " hailing from Florida.

" Look here," said I to Kizer one sharp December day, " all the antelope have left this range and I'm blessed if I'm going to live on bacon all winter."

Small wonder that they left after Rebel Jim sent in three hundred antelope carcasses to Colorado City in the first three weeks of September, all of which he killed with his telescope-sighted rifle within six miles of my Colorado ranch. I don't blame him. He was hunting for a living ; he got it too.

" In Texas," said Kizer, " when we was short of beef we mostly killed a maverick."

The herd with which he had come up had been camped far out on the Plains : he had never been in Colorado before.

" Colorado is not Texas," said I with emphasis.

" Colorado's too high-toned to let common fellers like you and me kill mavericks. We're not school trustees. Special law here assigns all such un-branded animals found at large to the trustees of the school fund."

" Well, what're ye going to do about it ? " said the cowboy. " Kill a stray ? There's a few un-gathered strays of the J J's left over as I've heard. Owner's gone back to Texas after selling out. You could offer to pay if you ever happened to meet up with him."

" H'm," said I. " There's a cowmen's vigilance committee in this county of El Paso that keeps their little eye open for that sort of thing. I might have to explain my action to a surprise party of masked gentlemen who came provided with a rope. No, I can't kill a maverick and I can't kill a stray, and I can't afford to kill one of my best steers, but I can tell you what I've made up my mind to do. You know that white bull of mine I showed you with the red ears—he's far too good a fighter to be popular round here, so we'll get him in and beef him. He'll be fat enough to be good meat, for he's had four months on the best buffalo grass in Colorado to fatten on since August."

So next day we rode out on the range to find the bull ; we had to hunt farther than we expected, for the bitter storms of winter had already begun and the cattle were much scattered. We found him however at last, along with his enemies of last summer, Randall's Durhams, peacefully feed-ing. Rivals who in summer thirst day and night

for each other's blood often chew the cud of peace side by side in winter, a picture of harmony.

We drove the whole bunch up to my corrals. Already a blizzard was coming down from the north. The sky had clouded over, the wind was biting cold, and flakes of snow began to fly.

" It'll be a freezing job to butcher him out here," said I ruefully to Kizer, as with numb fingers we put up the corral bars.

Kizer, whose heart was back in his own warm sunny south, agreed emphatically ; he loathed the Colorado climate.

"Look at here," I said. " I'll tell you what let's do. We'll open the door of the barn "—in the West a stable is called a barn—" and get him inside there to kill. It's warm in there out of this wind."

Kizer, who was already chilled to the bone by the rising Colorado zephyr, our pet name for a blizzard, joyfully agreed. We turned our horses loose to join the band ; we were not stabling any of them yet, for grass was good and the Western cow-pony of that day was bred able to fend for himself out of doors all the year round, and he often had to do it. We got the knives, and the gambrel-stick and a rope to sling him up by after he was shot, as well as an axe and a bowl of hot water for splitting and washing the carcass, and set them in a corner of the empty barn, while I put fresh caps on my six-shooter and belted it on. Our preparations were complete.

We threw open the door of the barn giving on

the corral with a view to driving the bull inside. The barn was some eight feet high to the eaves, with a loft above it, now stuffed as full of hay as it would hold, for we expected to feed hay to my dozen of cow-ponies, at least during the worst storms before spring. The barn had an eight-foot gang-way down the middle and three low-mangered double stalls on each side divided by strong pole partitions about five feet high.

Cautiously we went out into the big corral where the bulls, whom we had driven very quietly, were standing. Randall's four young shorthorns, part of the Sam Hertzel lot, were tame enough. But the white bull was prairie bred and could, I knew, be a bit of a handful if he liked. He was not a Spanish bull from Texas, spite of old Randall's base insinuations ; but, as I have said before, his red muzzle and ears showed that he threw back to the ancient white cattle of Great Britain, now represented only in the famous wild herds of Chartley and Chillingham, and in the occasional white speci-mens not rarely to be seen in the south-west of Wales. It is a noble breed truly, but better fitted to survive in the struggles of the prairie than of the show-yard.

We dodged around very quietly to avoid excit-ing the brutes, and more than once we had brought our quarry nigh up to the open door, but the son of the prairie had no use for barns and declined to enter. Already he began to grow uneasy : he suspected something and was anxious to escape from the corral.

" You go and open the far door of the barn,"
said I to Kizer, " and stand behind it. Then when
he comes to this door again and sees daylight through
the two doors he'll try to make a bolt for it. You
bang yours in his face and I'll shut mine behind
him and we'll have him nabbed."

No sooner said than done. Kizer opened the
far door, I manœuvred him again up to the near
one ; he thought he saw his chance for liberty
and made a dash through, only to find one door
slammed before him and the other behind ; a
bellow of dismay proclaimed that he was trapped.

The first part of our job was done ; Kizer came
round and we turned the other beasts loose ; then
we went to the barn. The bull was waiting quietly
inside.

" Who's going to shoot him ? " said Kizer.

Mostly I did it myself, and prided myself a little
that I never yet had had to shoot twice. But I
had heard great things of the Texas cowboy's shooting powers and on the impulse of an ill-starred
moment I said :

" Oh, you if you like," and I handed him the
gun.

She was an old muzzle-loading ·36 Colt—I have
given one just like it to the Oxford museum—but
she was never beat for straight shooting, and I
told Kizer so as I handed her over. Scott ! what
an idiot I was.

We peeped through the crack of the door—
the barn was very stoutly built of logs, but it was
not chinked all round and had a window on the

south, so it was pretty light inside. We could see the bull at the far end. Swiftly I slipped the bolts and we stepped silently in, Kizer in front, the pistol cocked in his right hand ; I bolted .the door behind us.

" In the curl as he turns," I whispered quickly. There is a curly lock of hair in the middle of a bull's forehead a bullet through which will find the brain.

And even as I whispered the bull turned, or rather spun rapidly round as if on a pivot. Up came the pistol which should have been raised before—there was a bang and then—well, what ought to have happened was the bull's twelve odd hundredweight of beef flat on the floor and us two running forward with the knives to bleed him. But what really happened next I never could precisely remember ; everything went so blamed quick. What I seem to see is Kizer and myself leaping, like scared cats, from mangers to the tops of partitions between stalls, while a mad bull with a bloody forehead chased first one and then the other of us from stall to stall like a terrier hunting rats. Never shall I forget the frantic terror of those breathless minutes, or the furious roars of the savage brute, while I felt his red hot breath on my hands as I squeezed across between partition tops and ceiling, followed by the rattle and crash of his horns against the strong partition poles as he struck viciously at me ; in dreams I still repeat my frenzied leaps across one stall and headlong scramble for the next partition while

the bull backed out and came round the corner
after me with a rush. The sense of utter impotence,
with a ghastly, horrible, violent death the instant
penalty of the least slip or slowness in scrambling,
was more hideous than I can say. It was like
the horrors of a nightmare come true.

Breathless, bruised and bewildered, sweat streaming off me, I paused at last for a moment's respite
on one of the partition tops : the bull had given
me a rest and gone for Kizer.

" Where's the gun ? " I shouted.

But Kizer, absorbed in his own frantic efforts
to escape the bull, heard nothing, took in nothing.

" Shoot him. Great Scott ! why don't you shoot
him ? " I bellowed.

Then as my wits collected themselves it dawned
on me that he must have dropped the pistol, for
he had no holster to put it into and needed to use
his hands in climbing. I looked on the floor and
sure enough there it lay in the first stall on the
opposite side. If I could only get at it. But
there was that broad gangway to be crossed in the
face of that raging monster. Well, it had to be
done. I dropped to the ground off my partition,
saw the bull in the far stall jabbing savagely up-
wards at Kizer, who was scratting over his partition
like a cat. With one bound I crossed the gang-
way, stooped, and rose again with the pistol in
my hand. Heaven be thanked, the hammer did
not jam, but came back with the pull of my thumb
and stood full cock. Would she miss fire ? I
had fears lest the bull might have stamped on it

and put it out of kilter, but there was no time now
to look, for he had spotted me and instantly backing out of the stall turned my way. As his head
came round I was glancing down the sights : my
special fancy was for the butt of the ear shot, but
the red hairy ear twitched swiftly past ere I could
pull trigger. Now the broad white face was straight
opposite me ; I caught the sight on the curl, and
bang she went. Thank goodness the pistol was
all right. Crash to the floor went the great white
bull, his legs jerking convulsively in the death
flurry.

It was all over. Kizer came down from his perch ;
we bled the carcass, wiped our steaming faces,
drew a few deep breaths, and chaffed one another
over our respective climbing powers as we fell to
work skinning, just as if five short minutes earlier
we had not been at hand-grips with imminent
death. I have faced the fury of a blizzard on the
Great Plains, I have been battened down on a
cattle-ship for thirty-six hours in the Western
Ocean while every hoof on deck was swept over-
board, I have sat helpless in the middle of a ring
of angry Indians while the debate raged whether
I should be put to the torture or not, but I think
the King of Terrors never came closer to me than
for five minutes on that short December evening
when all I was thinking of was which joint to select
for my Christmas beef.

As for my " mean white " cowboy, Mr. Kizer,
in truth I got pretty sick of him. He had the
name of being a good deal of a ruffian and this had

made it hard for him to get a job : in fact, I had taken him on partly out of pity. Now I let him know that as soon as spring came I should pay him off. He said no word to me about it, but he opened his mouth to some others.

" Look at here," said Tom Russell to me one day when we were camped together down on the Fountain looking up some strays. " You got to keep your eye skinned with that Kizer man you got working for you now. He's pretty low down and comes of a mighty mean stock. He's taken a spite against you, and he's told me he's going to whale hell out of you when you've paid him over what's coming to him. I tell you, he's tough and he'll bear watching."

I thanked Tom for telling me, and thought over what he had said as I lay in my blankets that night. I did most particularly hate the idea of a row with such a brute. He was thirty pounds heavier than I was, and knew all there was to know about such foul tricks as gouging and biting. I fixed it up with myself what to do, and then slept like a top.

In the morning I said to Kizer, " Lets you and me ride up the west side of the creek while Tom and his pal take the east side."

Off we went, and a mile or so from camp we came into a nice grove of cottonwoods with their white bark.

" Look at here," said I to Kizer, " you saw me kill that white bull in the barn, but I don't think I ever showed you how quick I could empty a six-shooter."

" No, I guess not," said he, looking at me suspiciously.

" Well, see now then ! " said I, jumping off my horse and dropping the reins over his head on the ground. I went to a good large tree trunk close by and cut a fair-sized mark on it with my butcher-knife. I came back a few yards, looking at him, then whirled and pulled my gun as quick as I could and loosed off the six shots in pretty quick time. All hit right in the mark or close to it.

" By God, you can shoot," said Kizer as he examined the shots, while I reloaded my pistol.

" Yes," said I, " and don't you forget it." Not another word passed, but when we got to the Springs and I paid him off he took his money like a little john man.

CHAPTER XVII

THE FATE OF THE MAVERICK

THE Texas shores of the Gulf of Mexico are bordered by a string of low islands, covered with rich grass, forming individually perfect little paradises for the stockman. At the time when the great Civil War between the Federals and the Confederates began, one of these islands belonged to a certain gentleman of the name of Maverick, who, like a chivalrous Southerner, went off to the front, leaving the cowboys to take care of his cattle. Ere long, however, the conscription was put in operation, the cowboys were swept in, and the cattle were left to take care of themselves. When Colonel Maverick returned to his island ranch four years later, on the conclusion of the war, he found that his cattle had run wild, and of course everything under four years old was neither marked nor branded. Accordingly he brought a host of cowboys over from the mainland to round them up, but the intended stock had grown wilder than buffalo, and when the cowboys hustled them out of the brakes the whole herd ran violently down into the warm waters of the Gulf and cheerfully swam away across the narrow strait to the mainland beyond. No sooner had

they landed than they proceeded to scatter over all creation and become mixed up with numberless other herds, and it took the poor Colonel years and years to collect them again. To the older cattle which had been properly branded he had, of course, a good title, but naturally his cowboys maintained whenever they came across an unbranded animal anywhere in the course of their wanderings that it was one of the younger members of the escaped herd; and malicious report had it that the Colonel's cows must all have given birth to triplets. Anyhow, the word to " maverick " passed into common use all over the West to signify the practice of seizing upon any stray animal, whether branded or not, that might or might not be yours. If it wasn't yours it was stealing to take it, but stealing is an ugly word, and people preferred to talk about " mavericking."

Under the peculiar conditions of life in the Far West it naturally behoved any man who went in for " mavericking " to be an extra good shot. It is popularly supposed that all men are dead shots out there, that almost anybody, in fact, can hit the exact button on your waistcoat that he wants to. My experience leads me to say that the ability is far from universal. Of course some men could do it right enough. Slade could, they said, and Sam Hildebrand and Buffalo Bill. I have seen Wild Bill pick up a peach can for practice and roll it along the ground, and then fire shot after shot into it, and keep it rolling till he had emptied his pistol. But men like that belonged

to the classiest order of desperadoes. The common man was nowhere alongside of them, and that was one reason why a man like Wild Bill could survive a hundred fights. Of course I don't deny that the average man out West is a useful shot, probably better than the average Boer ; still he can miss freely enough, even at close quarters, if he happens to be anyways rattled. And apropos of " mavericking," it was a " maverick " that was the occasion of some of the very worst pistol shooting I ever witnessed in my life.

We were at Jabe More's ranch on Big Sandy for the round-up. I suppose there were a hundred men assembled, and there may have been a couple of thousand head of cattle on the range. We rounded them up, and every ranchman cut out his own stock to take away, and then the range cattle were turned loose again. Now it so happened that among them was a certain stray animal, a huge red Texas steer. He wasn't Jabe's ; he wore several brands, that of the ZOZ in particular, and he was supposed to have escaped from a travelling herd that had passed through to Montana the year before. Accordingly all the respectable ranch-men left him alone, while every man there who was after " mavericks " had a good long look at the " critter " while he was in the round-up to see if he could find any mark or brand to which he might be able to set up the shadow of a claim. However, these gentry who were " on the make " were a trifle afraid of each other ; in short, that big ZOZ steer was too well known, and not one of

them ventured to cut him out. It made them feel pretty sick though to see that great long-horned sixteen-hand lump of fat beef lying around loose; he was just going to waste, so to speak; and many longing eyes followed him as he strung out along with the range cattle towards the hills. Most of the more respectable ranchmen had already moved away, when suddenly up spoke a man known as Jack Sheppard. It was generally understood that that wasn't his real name; also that he was about the coolest hand anywhere round at getting away with a cow whose brand was a trifle dim.

" Boys," laughed Jack Sheppard to his fellows, " I seed you all have a good look at that ZOZ steer, but there warn't a man that had the nerve to claim him and cut him out. Now you hear me talk! I claim him. That's my steer; and I'll butcher him for the benefit of the round-up."

A good many men laughed at this, partly seeing the humour of the situation, and partly feeling naturally cheerful at the prospect of fresh beef in camp.

" Right you are," Jack continued boldly, " and seeing as how nobody raises any objection I take it as how silence means consent. I'll jest sail in and rope him on my little mare, and then one of you fellers can shoot him."

It was a simple way of Jack's to spread the responsibility on other shoulders as well as his own. Away dashed the little mare full split into the open ranks of the dispersing cattle; the next

minute we beheld her returning at headlong speed, and the great red steer flying before her. Jack was swinging the noose of his rope round his head, but he waited till he was within fifty yards of us before he threw it. Then the noose shot forward, the spare coils slipping rapidly from his left hand; with beautiful accuracy it fell just over the great steer's horns, and as a flick of the wrist tightened it, the terrified brute leaped six feet into the air, bellowing wildly with fear and shaking his head in a vain effort to free himself. Not much chance of freedom for him though! Jack and the little mare knew their business too well for that. Jack's deft right hand swiftly took a turn of the rope on the horn of the saddle; while the little mare, ear and eye bent upon the steer, stopped short, and sticking out her forelegs sat down almost on her tail in readiness for the shock. It came; the wild, raging steer was brought up with a jerk, and the half-inch rope hummed like a taut bow-string as it was strained to the uttermost. She held him grandly, her forefeet ploughing up the dust, though he jerked her along, two yards at a time, in his frantic efforts to break away. He would have dragged a green horse over in a moment, but the mare knew well how to use her strength; the rope was new and sound, the saddle horn was of ironwood cased in raw hide; nothing gave, or was likely to give; and when the mare dug her toes in and set herself back, the steer was brought up short every time. But she weighed only some six hundred odd pounds, while the steer must have

been hard on to three-quarters of a ton; it was like lassoing a wild locomotive.

"Quick there, one of you," shouted Jack hastily to the crowd; "shoot him, somebody, and be quick about it."

That was where Jack slipped up: dropped his water melon, so to speak. He was just a trifle over-anxious. You see, here he was, with a highly excited steer bounding about only twenty-five feet from him at the other end of the rope; and he was at the same time somewhat oppressed by his moral responsibilities in thus making away with a stray. For, you understand, this act of his was really nothing less than cattle stealing; and some of the Bijou Basin cattlemen had hanged three men over on Kiowa Creek the year before for "mavericking" one measly calf that didn't belong to them. Of course, if the ZOZ brand hadn't now been a thousand miles away in Montana Jack would never have thought of doing such a thing thus publicly; but even as it was we saw that his mind was just a little bit distracted. What he ought to have done was to have named either Jack Hall or Tom Russell, men known as good shots and cool hands, to do the killing, and either of them would have done it all OK, while the rest looked on. But when Jack called out, "Shoot him somebody, quick!" then somebody—I never noticed who— pulled his gun instantly and shot. I judge that he shot for the butt of the ear, for the steer was sideways to where we stood, so that one couldn't see his forehead square; and it can't be denied

that his intention was right enough, for there's
no deadlier place to lodge a bullet than the butt
of the ear ; only unfortunately he didn't hit it.
The ball struck the steer somewhere over the eye,
and, glancing off the bone, didn't " phase " him
in the least, but he was wild with pain and fury,
and he leaped high in the air again, and ran out
his tongue a full foot, and bawled so loud that
many of the round-up cattle turned and answered
him from the hill ; in fact, I more than half thought
they were going to charge down on us.

" Great Scott ! " yelled Jack. " Can't you shoot
better than that ? "

A dozen men threw their right hands back to
their hips, out came a dozen revolvers, and " Pop,
pop, pop," they went, and " pop, pop, pop." Such
a scene I never saw. The maddened steer plunged
in wild leaps at the end of the rope, and bawled
louder than ever as fresh bullets stung him here
and there in the head and neck ; Jack's little mare
gamely hung on to him, but she was fairly stagger-
ing now under his desperate pulls, while the excited
men kept trying to get a quick aim on their rapidly
shifting target, and at the same time to avoid
hitting Jack or the mare. I suppose sixty or seventy
bullets were fired off in about a minute and a half,
but not one reached the brain, and the frantic
steer seemed stronger than ever.

" Will nobody take the rope from me ? " cried
Jack in despair. " This mare's about done."

And indeed it began to look as if she must fall
over now at every fresh jerk. In sailed Tom Russell

with a fresh horse and took the rope off Jack's horn and transferred it to his own, and that was a feat that called for both nerve and skill with that mad steer surging on the lasso. There came a lull in the firing then, for the pistols were empty; but now appeared Jabe More himself on foot, running fast from his shanty with a Spencer rifle in his hand. He slowed to a walk and cautiously advanced almost to the tail of Tom Russell's horse; the steer paused in his struggles for one instant, and in that exact instant Jabe planted a ·50 calibre ball right in the curl in the middle of his forehead. That did the business sure enough, and all that remained was to skin and cut him up. It didn't take long to do it either, for those men who had shot so shocking bad were all precious glad to lend a hand and play they were mighty busy, by way of avoiding being asked questions.

But I never saw a man so cross as Jabe More was.

" I'd have you know, Mr. Jack Sheppard, or whatever it is you call yourself," said he very abrupt, " that I don't want any strays ' mavericked ' on my range. The foreman of the ZOZ wrote me to look after that steer, and I reckon if you're wise you'll settle up for it in mighty short order. And there's another thing too, mister. Next time you want to beef a steer, don't come and do it close to my water-hole. To-morrow, when my cattle come stringing in to water, and the bulls smell that blood, they'll just be charging around and bellowing all up and down the creek and knock-

ing the face off each other instead of attending to business. You'd oughter know by this time that you can't hardly do a cattleman a worse mischief than go and spill blood close to where his cattle waters, and send them all plumb crazy to fight and tear round. 'Tain't that you're a green tender-foot, Mr. Jack Sheppard, and that you don't know better. The trouble with you is that you've got neither honesty nor manners about you."

This was mighty plain talk on the part of Jabe More, but he stood there with the Spencer in his two hands and six shots still in the magazine, and he looked like backing up every word he said. Of course Jack had his gun too, and he had it loaded at that, for he hadn't fired at the steer; so there were a good many who looked to see a fuss started right there, for Jack had always posed as a fighting man. But that wasn't his day out. The way Jabe had planted that bullet in the curl of the steer was discouraging, and it helped Jack to see he'd done wrong. He apologized on the spot. I didn't quite hear all the long rigmarole he went into, how he'd intended to write to the ZOZ foreman in Montana himself, and send him the money there direct, and explain all about it; and had never meant to inconvenience Mr. More in any sort of way by butchering a beef between his cabin and the water-hole; and so forth, and so on. But I know Jack ate humble pie, and that was enough for Jabe More, and there was no more shooting either at men or "mavericks" that day.

The round-up crowd ate the beef, and extremely good it was too. Yet I fear that not one of us but felt that the ZOZ man's chance of getting paid for that beef was slim, and sarcastic references to Jack Sheppard's seven-year-old " maverick," a " maverick " that was branded pretty well from his ears to his tail, were appreciated in the camps for some time afterwards.

Perhaps it was in retribution for the piece of ZOZ beef which I helped to eat in that camp that I myself a little later had to endure the ignominy of having to prove to a tenderfoot that I had not " mavericked " an old cow of his. It came about thus : it happened that I sold some cattle to a man who had a ranch up in the mountains, and among them was an old barren cow, a brindled, lop-horned Cherokee. I helped him to drive them to his place ; and we did not counterbrand, as I was parting with my whole herd at the time. We stopped for noon just at the gate of the mountains on the Clearwater, and turned the cattle loose to graze in the bottom, where there was a good deal of brush. After making our noon halt we started to gather them up again and go on ; but, lo ! the brindled Cherokee was missing. We hunted up, we hunted down, but all in vain. Neither hair nor horn of her was to be found. Close by was the entrance to Eagle Park, a mesa-walled valley which had recently been bought by General Hanlon, an Eastern millionaire who had brought his family out for their health's sake, and had erected a mansion here and enclosed the park. At the gate,

which was fastened, we saw his servant, a newly-imported arrival from England, who, like most tenderfeet, looked on all Western men as wild savages. We inquired if he had seen the cow, and he at once assured us that if we meant a brindled, lop-horned cow he had, and that, what was more, he had got her safe inside the fence, and meant to keep her.

" But why ? " I inquired in astonishment. " What claim do you make to her ? "

" She be our cow," was the reply, " one we be a-milking of that got away last week, and summun or other's been and ' mavericked ' her, as they calls it in this country. 'Tain't the name they calls it where I comes fro'," and he turned a very meaning glance at the pair of us.

I looked at my companion and he looked at me, and we both burst into a fit of laughter. We were both old ranchmen, and to have a cow that had worn my brand for four years taken away from under our very noses by this tenderfoot outfit, as the Eastern millionaire and his servant were styled, was really too funny. We laughed till we nearly fell out of our saddles. But the raw immigrant stuck to his post behind the gate and stoutly refused to deliver the cow—General Hanlon's cow, as he called it. My companion was a little inclined to ride over and take the cow *vi et armis* : perhaps he was less tickled by the humour of the situation than I was.

" Look here," I said, " this loony tenderfoot really believes that he's right and that we're a couple of cattle thieves. You go along to the

ranch with the cattle and I'll gallop down to town
—it's only two miles off—and swear out a writ
of replevin, and get Millard Stone "—he was the
sheriff—" and be ready to have that cow out of
there by the time you can get back. We'll run
up a pretty bill of costs for our millionaire friend
anyhow."

So we settled to do this. My companion started
on with the cattle, and I loped my pony into town,
found Judge Phinn at his office, swore out a writ
of replevin before him, giving double security,
found Millard Stone to serve the writ, and meeting
my companion on our way up to Eagle Park reached
the gate once more. We took the liberty of letting
ourselves in, and rode around through the park
searching for the cow, while the tenderfoot rushed
off to the mansion to acquaint his master with
the facts. General Hanlon was away, but presently
we saw a buggy, with Mrs. Hanlon in it, driven
by her servant, coming full speed after us. Mrs.
Hanlon was a lady well known for her high spirit
and decision of character.

"What do you men want here?" she cried as
soon as she was within earshot of us. "Don't
you know this is private property?"

"I'm the sheriff, madam," answered Millard
very politely and taking off his hat, "and I'm
here to execute a writ for a cow that these gentlemen claim."

"Well, you won't get her," said Mrs. Hanlon
with emphasis, and urging the buggy close behind
us she proceeded to utter a stream of very cutting

remarks about Colorado ranchmen and their ways of dealing with the cattle. " 'Mavericking,' they call it," she said, " and it's downright stealing and nothing less, and they're a pack of thieves the lot of them."

This hit Millard Stone as well as us, for he, or rather his father, was a cattle-man likewise, and owned the MF brand; but one can't talk back to a lady, and the three of us had to ride on sheepishly enough while Mrs. Hanlon rode behind and plied us with taunts and jeers. At last, to our great relief, we saw the cow, and setting spurs to our horses we left the buggy behind for a minute or two and proceeded to drive her. We could not, however, take her along at a gallop, as she would presently have turned to fight, and as soon as we slowed up Mrs. Hanlon came full tilt behind us, and her stream of invective began again. Our finding the cow redoubled her rage. Weren't we ashamed of ourselves, three great strong men, to come and steal a cow away from a poor woman whose husband was from home? Ruffians, robbers, rogues, no word was too bad for us. In moody silence we plodded on with this volcano of abuse pouring on our backs. At last Millard made an effort to appease her wrath. Turning half round in his saddle, he exclaimed, with the deprecatory air of a man in a disagreeable position who can't help himself :

" It's no use your going on like this, madam. You know it's the law and I've got to carry it out."

" Law ! " shrieked Mrs. Hanlon. " Don't you talk of the law to me ! I won't obey any laws I don't help to make ! " Woman suffrage had just been defeated at the polls in Colorado at the recent election, and Mrs. Hanlon was still chafing under the sense of defeat. " It's an abominable shame," she continued, " the men make the laws, and men, or wretches who call themselves men, execute them and give poor women no chance."

This was pretty hard on Colorado, the laws of which were indeed extraordinarily favourable to women in the matter of property. For instance, if a married woman owned real estate she could dispose of it absolutely at her own discretion, while a married man could not dispose of his without his wife's written consent. However, it is no use to argue with a lady in Mrs. Hanlon's frame of mind, and to her we were dumb.

" Look here," said Millard Stone to me when we got clear of the gate and silently took our farewell of Mrs. Hanlon, " next time you've got a writ for that outfit you get a deputy to serve it. I don't see being talked to like that for any two dollars and a half."

He put me in possession of the cow and made return of the writ to Judge Phinn, who appointed that day week for the hearing of the case, and both parties were cited to appear. On the day fixed, my companion and I turned up promptly, but to our surprise the tenderfeet did not put in any appearance at all. Judge Phinn of course decided for us, and gave us as much as the law allowed in

costs and witness fees (the amount did not cover half our expenses) ; and then the joke came out. The tenderfeet had found their own cow in the interval. She had been running on the mesas just above the park all the time, only they couldn't see her, and in their helpless ignorance they imagined that my TH brindled, lop-horned Cherokee, which happened to look very like her, was their own lost cow, and that my TH brand on her hip, which had been there for four years, had been put on fraudulently in the course of the last few days. I hope they were ashamed of themselves for their stupidity, for neither I nor my companion, nor the sheriff, are likely to forget the talking to we got from Mrs. Hanlon when she used her tongue to such effect in trying to prevent us from recovering my " maverick."

CHAPTER XVIII

THE KING OF THE PRAIRIE

OF old the buffalo bull was the king beast of the prairie. Who was there but man to dispute his sovereignty? The bull elk carried a pair of horns like the branches of an oak, and the mustang stallion could kick like a hurricane, but the buffalo bull weighed two thousand pounds as he stood in his tracks, and the biggest elk or mustang that ever stepped was as a child's toy beside him. Old Ephraim, the grizzly, might indeed have made a hard tussle for it with his terrible claws and fangs, but his surly strength mostly chose to expend itself in other directions; too many of his ancestors had had their ribs driven in by a pair of strong sharp horns set in a head of adamant for him to take any chances, and he preferred to give best to the bull buffalo without a fight. As for the rest of the animals, they followed the example of their betters, and left the king of the prairie severely alone, only the lank grey wolf sneaked in the rear of the herds, where battle and old age and lightning flash and tempest provided victims enough to keep the hunger-bitten scavenger of the prairies from starvation. And so the millions of buffalo lived on, proud and happy,

generation after generation, until the last quarter of the last century.

Then the white men built their railroads out into the heart of the buffalo country, and, armed with Sharpe's rifles and Winchesters, they poured forth in their thousands to finish him off. It took them scarce fifteen years to do it, but I am proud to think that I had neither part nor lot in that slaughter. I had my ranch and my cowboys and my herd of cattle, and that was good enough for me. What should I want to fly around for, trying to earn a few paltry dollars as a hide hunter, when from my hardy Texas cows and splendid shorthorn bulls I could raise year by year the very finest kind of improved steers to sell to the miners in the mountains. My cattle fattened themselves summer and winter on an untouched range forty miles across ; how could they help fattening when on Squirrel Creek they had the run of the very best buffalo and grama grass, the strongest and sweetest feed that ever grew out of doors. Thousands of buffalo grew fat there on it in the old days, and it was there that I ran on to the very last buffalo I ever saw or expect to see alive outside of a menagerie. There had been no buffalo in on the range for years, and that was a magnificent old bull whom I found absolutely alone. If I was no slayer of the buffalo I knew right well their nature and their ways, and I knew what had brought him there away from the rest of his kind. It was here on Black Squirrel Creek that his mother had borne him as a calf, and here first he had drunk at the clear cool springs and

cropped the short curly buffalo grass almost at the foot of Pike's Peak. From this range in the great migration of his tribe he had swung north to the Republican and the Platte, and south to the Arkansas and the Cimarron.

As he grew older he fought his way up in many a desperate struggle with rival after rival till he proudly trod the earth the unquestioned master of his band. His huge frame developed, and his thews and sinews became as iron. His great hump and neck and head were clad in a rough mass of shaggy mane, the wealth of his thick dewlap almost swept the ground. His reign lasted many a long year, and he was every inch a king. But lately there had come a day—as it must come to all of us—when his muscles were less elastic and his breath was shorter than of yore. That day a younger bull—one of his own sons perchance— now in the very prime and flower of his age, equal to the monarch in weight and strength, superior in quickness and in wind, had challenged him to mortal combat. They had fought for hours, round after round, pushing and thrusting, butting and horning, till both were fairly spent and almost foredone. But youth will be served, as they say in the ring; the younger lasted longer and came off victor in the end.

Deeply the vanquished champion felt his dis- grace: before the very eyes of his cows and of his heifers he saw himself put to utter shame. Sullen and savage he withdrew, and spent the night alone for the first time, nursing his wrath. To-morrow

he would be rested ; to-morrow he would seek his insolent rival again, and he would win, or else die fighting, fit end for a warrior. To-morrow came, and the combat was renewed. Alas, for the old hero ! he could neither win nor die. For the second time his more youthful and vigorous rival fought him to a standstill, and left him helpless and exhausted, yet with his life whole in him yet. The triumphant victor moved off proudly over the hill accompanied by the faithless band ; the fallen champion saw himself deserted, and he laid himself down longing for the death that would not come. There as he lay thoughts of his lusty youth came back to him ; he remembered the cool springs of Black Squirrel Creek and the sweet pastures where he was born, and he desired to taste of them once more. There was virtue for him in those crystal waters, and with the strong rich grama oats of the sand-hills he would renew his youth ; his lost vigour would surely come back ; after that he would return once more and find the band— his band—and then the presuming upstart who had supplanted him should learn what he still could do. With the thought he felt his strength revive a little ; he struggled to his feet ; he turned his shaggy front towards Black Squirrel Creek ; never since his calf-hood had he forgotten the exact direction in which lay the place where he was reared ; and thitherward he pushed steadily ahead. And stealthily behind him and on either flank skulked half a dozen lank grey buffalo wolves, following. He did not condescend to notice them. He had

disdained them all his life : why should he now stoop to give them a thought ? He did not consider that now for the first time he was alone, stiff and weak from his great battle, with a red gash on his side left by his rival's horns, nor did he know that the hungry wolves had smelt his blood. On, on, he pushed, following an old and once well-travelled road that in their migration the buffalo had made ; it ran from the Republican to Big Sandy, from Big Sandy to Rush Creek, and from Rush to Black Squirrel Creek ; the latter part of it was grass-grown now, but his instinct led him true. And ever as he went the wolves went also ; there were more of them continually, and continually they grew bolder, closing in upon their prey. Big Sandy had long been left behind, Rush Creek was passed, and the edge of the Black Squirrel Creek ranges was gained. He stopped to taste the first bite of the pastures of his youth. Pah, they were dry and dusty now. What was it that had changed ? Could it be he ? And the tireless wolves drew nearer still, and lay down to rest themselves and get ready for the end. They would need all their strength for the final onset.

But the end was not to be quite as they imagined, for over the hill on a sudden there came a man riding alone. The bull did not see him, for his shaggy front-let half-concealed his eyes ; the wolves saw him, however, and were on their feet in an instant ready for flight. The solitary horseman was myself, and this was how I came to be there.

It was early spring, and wherever the ground was

a little moister or the air a trifle warmer than elsewhere the sweet fresh young feed was just beginning to start. My band of saddle horses, sick and
tired of the old dry last year's grass on which they
had grazed all winter, went plumb crazy for a bite
of the tender sprouts of the new growth, and deserting their wonted haunts by Holcombe Hollow
they hunted eagerly for green grass all over the
country. And so it came about that I presently
missed two of them, nor was it hard to guess that
they had wandered away southwards where the
grass started earlier. My two cowboys were busy
breaking in some colts, so I left my books—we cattle-
men are not all savages, and I read a great deal
in winter—and, saddling up, I started out alone
to look for the runaways. I searched all day without seeing a sign of them, and that night, of all
places in the world, I slept at MacTaggart's sheep
camp. Cattle- and sheep-men, as a rule, agreed
about as well as buffaloes and wolves, for where
the sheep graze the cattle die. In the early days
we pioneers had boldly pushed out on to the great
ranges with our Texas herds, and we felt ourselves
to be every bit as much the lords of the prairie as
ever the buffalo had in the past. But now that
our cowboys had taught the Indians to keep at a
respectful distance, and made the country comparatively safe, these sneaking sheepmen were
beginning to creep in, digging wells where they
liked on Government land, and squatting right in
the heart of our best cattle grazing. Were we, too,
to follow the buffalo and be driven out ? Was

our day of doom at hand? There were cattle-men who said "No" to that, who resisted by violence, who went at night and stampeded flocks of sheep, and fired into the houses of their owners. But I was not one of them. The sheep-men were within their lawful rights, and I myself was a law and order man, first, last, and all the time. Perhaps a little earlier I might have kicked, when I was still young and my blood was hotter. But now that I have grown older I see more and more clearly that Fate will have its way, and that the new order of things is always being built up on the ruins of the old. Well, well. Kismet! Let it come, say I.

And so I went to MacTaggart's. I had seen him once or twice already in The Springs, but I had avoided his shanty; the sight of it in the distance was enough to sicken me, for on my range he was the first invader. A rank tenderfoot he was, a great, red-faced, beefy sort of man, a British colonist, hailing from that very out-of-the-way spot in the Gulf of St. Lawrence known as Prince Edward's Island. Well, I had no objection to him on that ground, as I was from the old country myself, and on the spur of the moment I accepted his invitation to stop the night when I met him about a mile from his shanty. He was on his way out from The Springs and he had a pair of really fine young American mares hitched to his waggon that it would do anyone's heart good to see.

"Lost your horses, heh?" said he in a rallying voice, when I told him how I came to be there. "That's what you cattle-men are always doing,

heh ? I cut hay for mine, and keep 'em tied close round home. Safe bind, safe find, heh ? "

I wanted a new name for cheek. Was this confounded tenderfoot going to teach a frontiersman how to manage his horses ?

" Can't do that sort of thing when you've got twenty cow-ponies," I said briefly. " You can't tuck 'em up in bed every night at home when you've got to ride hundreds of miles on the round-ups after your stock."

" Wouldn't suit my constitution," laughed the fat-faced flock-master. " Don't care about riding much, nowise. Nay, I don't so much as own a saddle. Not but what I used to gallop around in the pasture on the plough-horses when I was a boy on the farm." He certainly didn't look much like a horseman as he sat there with an old army blanket rolled round him on the spring seat of the farm waggon.

" A man had better be able to ride," I said. " Yes, and to shoot, too, if he's going to live in the Far West. He never knows the day when he mayn't want to do one or t'other, and if he does he'll want to do it powerful bad, as a Cheyenne City gentleman said to me once."

" Well, as for shooting, I've got a scatter gun," he returned. " Does to kill these long-eared jackass rabbits with first-rate, and that saves my mutton, d'ye see. And then one of the Jackson boys has a revolver."

The Jackson boys were twin brothers whom he had got to come out from the island to work for

him at twenty dollars a month. If the Mac in his name meant that he was of Scotch blood, he certainly did no discredit to his ancestry. He was canny if ever a man was, and the idea of paying men what I paid my Colorado cowboys, forty dollars, would have made him feel sick.

The Jackson boys had just corralled the sheep for the night as we reached the shanty. They really were the two very finest young fellows I ever laid eyes on. Each twin was as like the other as two peas, and " six feet four and as broad as a door " was about their mark for size. It warmed my heart, even if they were tenderfeet, and sheep-herders at that, to see their friendly faces and listen to their innocent talk. I had got into the habit of thinking that everybody in North America was born, so to speak, with a gun in his hand and a six-shooter in his hip pocket, and it was quite a relief to run across these Arcadian youngsters who knew precious little of firearms and nothing at all of bloodshed. They had come from a quiet, decent, law-abiding district, where shooting scrapes and Indian fights had scarcely been heard of except in story-books, and I vainly tried to make their hair stand on end by telling them what the Cheyennes had done when they raided us three years back. I might picture all the horrors of the scalping knife and the stake ; but they were armed in a happy unconsciousness that made them proof against qualms.

" We've seen Indians at home," said the younger twin. " There's plenty of Micmac hunters in the

woods ; and there's bears too ; why, Brother Will
here killed a bear with his axe last fall."

"Yes," said I, "and ten of your little black
bears wouldn't make one Rocky Mountain grizzly.
And as for your Micmac hunters—well, if the
Cheyenne Dog-soldiers ever run on to you when
you're herding sheep, you'd better get into a buffalo
wallow with a Winchester or they'll have you
on toast."

Within an hour after I left them next morning
I began to think that I had found a Cheyenne
warrior myself when I came in sight of a solitary
black object more than a mile away that at first
I took to be nothing less than an Indian sitting
bent forward over the neck of his mount. A cattleman scorns to run from a single Indian, and I rode
towards him, not without caution though, for there
might be more of them about, but unseen. And
then of a sudden I made out that what I had taken
to be the bent back of a man on horseback was
nothing else than the great hump of a solitary
old buffalo bull.

Under cover of the hill I rode undiscovered
to within eighty yards, and gazed at him awhile.
He stood motionless, a lonely and majestic survivor,
type of the era that was so swiftly passing away.
I read his history, even as I gazed, in his great
head hanging low, and in the long red gash upon
his scarred side. And then I caught sight of the
wolf pack lying down in the grass and waiting. I
knew well what that meant. As soon as the pinch
of hunger gave them courage to attack, they would

make a combined rush at him ; the more cunning ones would bay him in front, always avoiding his irresistible charge and the fierce toss of those wicked horns, till at last the boldest of the cowardly lot seizing his opportunity, and springing on the victim from behind, with one tearing snap of his terrible wolfish fangs, would cut the hamstring ; and behold, the ex-monarch of the prairie crippled and help-less ! Last of all, I saw in my vision the fall of the monarch, the disembowelling alive and the gruesome feast of victory. Every detail of the cruel scene printed itself on my brain, while I watched their slinking steps as they rose. Should I baulk them ? Should I end his career by a merciful bullet ? But I had robes and meat enough at home already. " No, old warrior," quoth I, " you shall go unharmed for me. Live as long as you can, and the wolves shan't get you yet if I can help it." With that I suddenly drove spurs to my pony and dashed full speed over the brow of the hill straight at them. The wolves and their prey were equally taken by surprise. Away fled the buffalo in the curious rocking gallop of his kind, and as Fate ordained it he took a line for MacTaggart's ranch, while the hungry wolf pack scattered before me like a frightened covey of partridges before the swoop of a falcon. I wasted half a dozen pistol-shots just for the fun of seeing them stretch themselves, but I could not afford to waste horse-flesh in riding them down, so I presently left them and turned once more to renew the search for my lost stock. The buffalo bull was already out of sight.

As luck would have it I ran on to my two strays a few hours later, and brought them at evening back to the sheep ranch. When I rode up I noticed that the sheep were already corralled, and the two young giants were kneeling, very busy over something or other, up on top of the shanty. As I came close I saw that they were stretching an immense green buffalo hide which covered the whole roof. Then I knew.

" Man," said the younger twin, looking down at me over the eaves, " but you had ought to have been along with us here to-day! We've had a grand time entirely. We've killed a great big buffalo."

" So I see," said I, " and I'm wondering to myself how you managed to do it among you."

" Oh, it was a grand fight," he answered, grinning, " and the boss come mighty nigh being killed."

" How did it all happen ? " I said, getting down to shift my saddle on to a fresh horse.

" Why, Brother Will was out with the sheep this morning," said the young tenderfoot proudly, " when he saw a great black thing as big as an elephant coming over the hill. At first he didn't know what to think of it, and then he guessed it must be a real live wild buffalo. So he left the sheep, and he ran to camp, and halloed to me and the boss that over yonder there was a buffalo bull as big as a house. And the boss unhitched the team, and stripped off the harness all but the blind bridles ; and he gathered the scatter gun and put two loads of buckshot in it, and jumped bare-back on one of the mares, and lit out for the buffalo.

Me and my brother fetched a surcingle, and rolled up a blanket so as to make a good pad, as there's no saddle on the place, and we girthed that on to the other mare, and then he took his revolver and lit out after the boss. I followed on foot, and just as soon as I come in sight of them over the hill, I saw the boss go galloping up to the buffalo, and he loosed off the first barrel of the shot-gun, and I guess he missed him clean. But the team mare wasn't used to being shot off, and she give a big plunge sideways, and the boss rolled right off on to the ground, and the buffalo see'd him there and come at him. And right as he lay, without getting up—for he was a goodish bit shaken—the boss slung the gun across his thigh and loosed off again and hit the buffalo, as he came up, in the near foreleg, and that charge of buckshot broke the bone, and the buffalo was sort of turned aside so that he missed his charge. Then the boss scrambled on to his feet and started to run away, but the buffalo came after him on three legs and caught up with him in a moment. Man, it was grand to see! The boss saw that the near leg hung loose, so he turned sharp to the left and ran in a little circle, and the buffalo kept circling after him. That near foreleg being broken, the buffalo had hard work to turn, and as long as the boss could whirl short to the left, the bull's horns missed him every time. But it was just nip and tuck, I can tell you, and the boss is a big fleshy man, and he soon gets short of wind. Three minutes more and I guess the buffalo'd have got him. But then came my brother on the other

mare, and he hung on tight to the surcingle with one hand for fear she'd jolt him off, and with the other he loosed off all six shots out of the revolver at the old bull, and the very last shot went into his lungs, and he fell down and bled at the mouth, and died. And you'd have laughed to see the boss set down beside him and puff and pant and snort and blow. Fair tuckered out, he was. But, man, what a monstrous size a buffalo is ! I reckon it took us nigh three hours to skin him and cut him up ; and then the boss put strychnine in the offal for the wolves, and started straight off to peddle the meat around in town, ' Poor as it is,' says he, ' 'twill fetch three cents a pound in The Springs, and the four quarters will weigh a thousand pounds. I'll net thirty dollars.' "

Thrifty MacTaggart !

By this time I had shifted my saddle on to one of my runaways, and now I swung myself into the seat, and driving the two loose horses before me I started for my night ride homewards. Dimly through the gathering dusk l saw the hungry grey wolves busy over the poisoned entrails as I passed the spot where the king of the prairie had fallen.

" Good night, old hero," I sighed, " your day is over ; your time had come ; all my good-will could not give you an hour's longer life ; it did but hasten your end. I reckon my day is pretty nigh over too. The cattleman is no more wanted here than the buffalo, and these tenderfeet look on one as pretty nearly as wild as the other. You faced the Indians and the wolves and the blizzards for many a day

before your time came ; so we cattlemen have borne
the brunt of it, and now we are to give place to a
set of creeping sheep-herders who can neither ride
nor shoot. And yet, old warrior, they are successful ; they cover their roof with your hide, they
make your offal bait for wolves, and they sell your
meat for thirty dollars in the market-place.

" But, after all, does the success belong to these
men ? Was it the strength of your own sons that
drove you out of the herd to die alone ? Was it
not old age that tamed your strength, the inevitable
fate against which even the gods strive in vain ?
And is it not the same inevitable fate that drives
me forth, and not these men who are my brothers ?
I cannot fight them, they are but the blind tools
of destiny, the forefront of the crowds that are
rolling westward with as irresistible an impulse
as that which ruled the migration of the buffalo
herds. The flood of men will sweep onward, and
in their turn farmers with their ploughs will come
to oust these shepherds as they have ousted me.
Each one of us has but—

> " A moment's halt, a momentary taste
> Of being, from the well amid the waste ;
> And lo ! the phantom caravan has reached
> The nothing it set out from. . . .

" And we men can see the doom coming, and
cannot avert it nor struggle against it. For the
end is denied to me that was granted to you   One
thing, old warrior, I envy you, and one thing only.
You died fighting, and that was what your great
heart desired."

CHAPTER XIX

THE BIG YELLOW STAG

TEXAS cattle just poured into Colorado in the early seventies. The millions of buffalo were being killed off or driven away, and the wild Indians who lived on buffalo had to go too. So here were tens of millions of acres of fine feed open to all the world. Among the cattle droves that came up from Texas was the Strong and Starbuck herd from the Nueces country in the west of the State. Also there came to Colorado Springs from the East a man with whom I became great friends. This was Colonel Wm. T. Holt of Maine. He had developed lung trouble, and that was what brought him to Colorado. He bought a good house in The Springs—he had lots of money—and settled into it with his wife and family. That house of his to me became a perfect godsend. I went there every time I came into The Springs, and found in it an atmosphere of affection and gentle companionship to which I had been pretty much a stranger since leaving home. All were so kind to me, and the change from the cow-camps was delicious. Meeting such dear people made a great difference to my last year in Colorado.

But Colorado air which did so much for Colonel Holt's lungs stimulated him also in another way. He was a man of vigorous physique and much energy. He could not see why he should not become a big cattleman as well as other people. So he proceeded to buy out Nash's little sheep ranch, which lay twenty-five miles beyond my place on the head of Horse Creek. Here he decided to build good cattle corrals and everything else needful, but before they were even begun he got the chance to buy out the Strong and Starbuck herd, and he took it. Then came the question of where to brand them, and I made the offer of the use of my corrals and branding shoot. It was promptly accepted, and the Texas men who had to do the branding—Holt wisely had stipulated for that— did the job there at my place. It was their job, so I and the two Mexicans I had working for me then had nothing to do but look on ; I tallied for Holt, and did everything I could think of to help him.

One of the two Mexicans working for me was Gus, whom I have already mentioned as Tom Russell's partner. They had dissolved partnership now, and Gus had left Randall and come to work for me. The second, Vicente Elias, was a good deal younger than Gus, but, like him, hailed from Old Mexico and showed in mind and appearance even more of the old Spanish stock. There is a well known picture by Velazquez of a Cavalier with his hand on a favourite wolf-hound's head that is singularly like Vicente.

But both men were markedly of the Latin race, courteous, high-spirited; their very faults were romantic. The contrast between them and the young Anglo-Saxon cowboys I had been living among made them extraordinarily attractive to me. Both men were courageous. Vicente indeed was a bit of a dare-devil. I remember his trying to lasso a mountain lion we ran across in the Spanish Peaks.

I quickly slid into friendliness and then into friendship with these men, and they, for their part, seemed to take to me.

However, while the Strong and Starbuck outfit were branding that Texas herd in my corrals, Gus and Vicente had their own work to do in riding around the range and looking after my stock.

It was no small job, the branding of those Strong and Starbuck cattle; but I had such a good crush-pen and corrals that it went far easier than one would have thought. There was no lassoing to be done: every single head was run through that crush-pen and felt the red-hot iron there. No, I am wrong. One and one only did not go through; and that was the Big Yellow Stag.

" Oh-h-h, Charley! Fetch up that last lot of steers for the crush-pen, will you? " shouted Jimmy Murray, making a speaking-trumpet of his hands as he sat there on his buckskin pony outside the bars of my big corral.

The buckskin pony was a yellow dun with black bars on his legs and a broad black stripe down his back.

They were just finishing off the job of branding the Strong and Starbuck herd, and Jimmy Murray, the foreman of the herd, bossed the job. He had brought the herd all the long three months' journey over the Goodnight Trail from Texas, and now he and his weary cowpunchers were keen to make an end of their labours and find their way back to their beloved sunny South before snow began to fly on the bleak plains of Colorado.

The Texas men didn't like Colorado.

" What do you wear shaps for in this country ? " I heard Bill Means, a youthful Colorado cowpuncher, innocently inquire of Jimmy at their first meeting.

Shaps were a sort of cowhide armour that all cowboys were compelled to wear in Texas to protect them from the terrible mesquite thorn, a defence which seemed hardly necessary on our treeless plains.

" What for ? " retorted Jimmy scornfully. " Why, to keep me from freezing to death in a climate where it's nine months winter and three months very late in the Fall."

Bill Means had wilted right there, and after that we none of us wondered that Jimmy Murray should look so pleased over the prospect of bringing the branding job to an end as soon as Arizona Charley and the boys fetched up the last lot of steers. Tall, gaunt, long-horned brutes the Strong and Starbuck steers were, bred in the thickets of the Nueces and the Palo Verde. They had been wild as hawks when they first started, but the long journey had tamed those wild hearts of theirs

a little, and a horseman could drive them now readily enough anywhere on the open prairie; yet the inside of a corral was strange and alarming to them still : some of them had never seen the inside of a corral but once before in their lives, when they were run in from the brush to endure the branding-iron and the knife before starting over the trail.

Hunched close together in their fear, excitedly snuffing and snorting, the last lot were brought up to the bars, Jimmy Murray on the buckskin pony circling round behind them to assist Charley and the others. Under pressure from the horsemen in their rear they were squeezed through the entrance ; the bars were hastily put in place, and we had the last lot of steers safe in the corral, the horsemen entering with them.

The next move was to draft them from the big corral through a gate into the little corral, not more than fifty feet across, which was the antechamber to the crush-pen.

The wild scary creatures, finding themselves trapped in the big corral, ran all round it, smelling at the fence and looking for a way out, until they came to the open gate. There they paused, snorting once more their distrust. Was this really an exit, or was it the entrance to a second trap ?

Close on their heels with shouts and cries the horsemen pressed ; with a leap and a bound the leading steer, hardening his heart, sprang through the opening, and after him sprang the rest, all but one, who roared an angry refusal and broke

resolutely back : he was a big bull-necked stag, the terror of the herd. Stag is the Texas name for a steer who has escaped the attentions of the cowboys during his youth, and this particular one had run wild as a bull in the Nueces thickets till he was six or seven years old ; his rusty sides showed the scars of many a pitched battle with his rivals, and he had the heart of a warrior in him still. He was built for a warrior too. He stood fully seventeen hands to the top of his huge buffalo-like shoulders, and his formidable horns were as thick as a man's arm and as sharp as daggers.

When the stag whirled and broke back Jimmy Murray whirled too, and chased him round the big corral, sending the buckskin pony flying up to his quarter, and calmly slashing the fugitive across the loins with the end of his lasso.

It was a treat to see Jimmy Murray ride. The easy seat, a little far back in the saddle, with the body perfectly upright, but giving freely to every motion of the quick-twisting cow-pony, was simply the perfection of balance. The pony, guided by hand and heel, turned and twisted, stopped or started on, exactly as if it was a part of him, automatically controlled by his brain. Jimmy never even seemed to think about his horse ; every few hours he mounted a fresh one, but apparently he took no account of any difference between one or another. He bestraddled indifferently anything that wore hair ; once in the saddle he treated it as if it were a mere machine that supplied him with an additional set of legs, and for him the

buckskin pony was but the most obedient of his willing slaves. One might almost have been looking at a centaur, the man and horse were so completely one.

Centaur-like though they were, I fully expected to see the big yellow stag turn on them when he felt the blow of the lasso, and send the pair of them flying together through the air with a toss of those tremendous horns; but no, he was not fighting mad yet; his most pressing desire so far was only to find a way of escape. He found none, however, though twice he made the circle of the big corral, and then, as he caught sight once more of his fellows in the little corral, gregarious instinct got the better of his fears and he suddenly bolted in after them. In, too, along with him went Jimmy Murray and the pony, the gate was shut behind them, and the last act began.

The other horsemen brought their steeds out of the big corral, and quickly hitching them, ran to the side of the crush-pen into which Jimmy with voice and lasso-end was forcing as many of the reluctant steers as it would hold. As soon as it was jammed full, strong poles were stuck across it behind the last animal so that none could back out; then the branding-irons were fetched, and in another minute there arose a strong odour of burnt hide and of frizzling hair, and the air rang with frantic bellowings, until finally the end gate of the crush-pen was opened and the terrified beasts were suffered one by one to escape. Colonel Strong and I sat upon some boards laid across the top

of the pen, carefully tallying each animal as it emerged.

No sooner were they all out and all tallied than the door of the crush-pen was closed, and Jimmy Murray shoved the other half of the bunch in to share the fate of their predecessors, a fate to which all went in gaily except the big yellow stag. That gentleman's suspicions had been aroused by the odour of the branding process and the bellowings of the sufferers, and he hung back.

Round and round the little corral he hurried, his head close to the ground, as if he were smelling at the bottom of the fence to find a weak place to burst out at, and from his throat there came a succession of low, short, ominous roars. He blew from his nostrils such strong blasts upon the ground that the pulverized dung which formed the floor of the corral sprang up in jets before him as he went.

Quite unmoved, Jimmy and the buckskin pony jogged round close behind his tail, Jimmy gently swinging his lariat and cheerfully chirruping to the monster. Jimmy's head was carried the least thing more proudly than ever ; caged in here with this savage brute, alongside which his pony looked like a toy horse, and almost within arm's length of those tremendous horns, one stab from which could have impaled horse and rider, Jimmy did not deign to show the faintest trace of anxiety. There was something almost ostentatious in the way in which his eye seemed to disregard the threatening terror just before him, and to be busily engaged

in overseeing the whole business of the branding,
as he took careful note how far each of the hands
was doing his work just right.

" Look out there, Jimmy ! " cried Colonel Strong,
" that big stag'll fight in a holy minute."

Jimmy, whose steady chirrup never ceased as
he jogged round, whether his eye were on the stag
or not, at last condescended to intermit his watch
on the branders and observe his adversary closer.

" I reckon he's not red-hot yet," he remarked
carelessly, " he's only blowing off steam a bit."

And he touched up the stag lightly with a swing
of the lariat, at which the big brute bounded forward and flung his head round threateningly ;
but, though he threatened, he did not charge.

" Just fly round there and open that gate,"
called out Colonel Strong to the branders. " Hurry
up, one of you, and let him back into the big corral."

He spoke loud, but the branders, conscious that
Jimmy Murray's eye was on them, and intent
each man on keeping his hot iron steadily pressed
upon his particular victim so as to avoid making
a blotch instead of a brand, seemed not to hear.
The stag had once more resumed his sulky circuit
of the fence, but those ominous short roars were
coming quicker and quicker. Jimmy's face was
as impassible as ever.

" Hi ! there, you Charley," shouted Colonel
Strong again, " don't stand there like a wooden
man. Jump, will you ? "

" Don't you talk like that to me, Colonel Strong,
'cos I ain't a-goin' to stand it," retorted Arizona

Charley sharply, removing his iron from a steer and looking up. "I'm a white man, I am, and I don't allow no man to talk to me like as I was anybody's doggoned nigger."

Jimmy Murray's chirrup ceased for a moment, and his cool voice turned the incipient dispute aside.

"Dry up, Charley," said he, "that'll keep. Best thing you can do is to let some of them branded ones out of the front of the crush-pen and make a bit more room, so as to give me the chance to cram this joker in behind the others."

But to me it looked as if, before all this could be done, the big yellow stag would surely be spilling Jimmy Murray's heart's blood on the floor of that corral. The Colonel's plan seemed the quickest; I jumped down and ran and opened the gate between the two corrals. The big stag instantly went through with a bound, turning his head and giving a snort like a fog-horn as he detected me where I stood behind the gate.

"That's a warrior, Jimmy," I called out to him as I climbed back to my exalted perch so as to be ready to help to tally out the branded lot. "You're mighty well quit of him."

Jimmy's firm-set mouth relaxed as he looked up at me with a friendly smile.

"He'll likely fight now," he said. "I doubt we'll not get him so near the branding-pen again, but we'll fix him yet one way or another; we're bound to get him branded and tallied, and if he won't come to the crush-pen I'd like jes' to show you

for oncet the way we set about tackling such gentry as him down in Texas."

It proved to be as Jimmy said. No persuasion now could induce him to enter the little corral a second time. As soon as some of us tried to go around him on foot he turned to fight in an instant, and hunted us to the fence, and then stood at bay on the far side of the big corral.

By this time the last lot in the crush-pen had been duly branded and tallied, and there remained only the big stag. We all gathered at the bars of the big corral, and the Coloradans looked forward with interest to see how the Texas men would work it. In those early seventies the Texans were the crack cowboys of the day. We hoped to see a really scientific display of lassoing, an art at which they were past-masters.

"Your cowpunching job's done, little buckskin," said Jimmy Murray to his horse as he dismounted outside and slackened the cinch. " ' 'Rah for the back-trail to Texas ' is what you can sing now. No more dry old bunchgrass in yours. 'Rah for growing fat again on pea-vines and mesquite."

The sweating pony shook himself all over as if he understood his master. It was the first time I had heard Jimmy speak caressingly to a horse. He was as brave as they make them, but he was as hard as the nether millstone.

Bill Means felt disappointed to see the cinch being slackened.

" Why, ain't you going to try and rope that stag on the little buckskin ? " he said to Murray, who

was standing with his lariat coiled over his arm.
" Or was you meaning to rope him on foot ?   I
guess, when you get to trying to hold him, it'll
be like snubbing an ironclad."

" I'll see if I can't show you a trick worth two
of that," said Jimmy, and leaving his horse to stand
he walked round the outside of the corral till he
was in sight of Colonel Strong's waggon, which
was encamped a little way off down by the creek.
He put his hands funnelwise to his mouth and
called aloud in high musical notes : " Yo-i, yo-i,
yo-i there !   Smiler, Sweetlips, 'Possum, you 'Possum ! come along then, come along ! "

With a joyful chorus of answering cries all the
dogs of the Texas camp came rushing over to his
well-known voice.   They were a motley pack, tykes
of sorts, black and tan foxhounds mostly, with a
fierce bloodhound cross in some of them, and there
was one, a mighty, deep-jowled, half-bred Cuban
mastiff, old 'Possum, the champion of them all.
They crowded around Jimmy's leather-guarded legs,
their red mouths and slavering lips welcoming the
summons, their eager muzzles snuffing the fray ;
at his call they seemed game to go at anything,
from a rabbit to a man-hunt ; we Coloradans wondered if they were really used for that down in
Texas.

Rope in hand, Jimmy stepped through the bars
into the corral, his pack crowding in alongside.

" S-sick him then," he cried, pointing to the big
stag over by the far fence.

Full speed across the corral streamed the pack,

giving tongue in short joyous yelps, and with one thundering roar the great brute lowered his head and rushed headlong to meet them. As they encountered, I saw Jimmy dart forward, single-handed, to take his part in the *mêlée*. The dogs divided as they met the stag, who, with rapid lunges of his powerful horns, struck out at them to right and left; but the pack were too nimble for him; his fierce thrusts missed their aim, and the next instant they were hanging on him in festoons, and 'Possum's, old 'Possum's, jaws were fastened like a vice in the very tenderest part of his flank. At that sharp pinch and the mastiff's mighty pull the great stag's loins sank and gave, and in a moment Sweetlips had him by the ear and Smiler by the cheek; he yielded to their united strain, and with a resounding thump came side-long to the ground; the dogs had fairly pulled him down. In a second Jimmy was alongside and slipped the noose around his hind legs, and then the other herders came up and tied him fast, drag-ging off as quickly as they could the infuriated hounds, who in another minute would have torn their prey to pieces.

Gasping, roaring and struggling, but all in vain, the terror of the herd lay helpless as a newly born calf; the hot iron was brought and pressed upon his hide, an outrage to which he could only reply by a bellow of impotent rage. Then he was duly ticked off on the list and tallied, and the transfer of the whole Strong and Starbuck herd was complete. Now, at last, Jimmy Murray's task was ended

or, at the least, it was all but ended, for only one thing remained to make it complete—the bound and prostrate stag had yet to be turned loose.

Jimmy stood by the back of his fallen foe with one foot planted on his heaving side.

"Look out there!" he cried. "You'd better clear out of the corral, all of you. And don't forget to put up them bars, somebody."

The man who was carrying the branding-iron retired at a run and put up the bars. The rest of us climbed the high corral fence and sat on top to see what the stag would do.

With the end of his rope Jimmy bent a clove-hitch round the stag's hind fetlocks and pulled it taut. Then, stooping cautiously over him, he untied and slackened the rest of his bonds till they were all loose. The stag lay quiet, but breathing hard, till he suddenly became aware that the cords had been relaxed, whereupon he made a violent convulsive effort that half-raised him from the ground. Lightly Jimmy rose up, and with rapid strides reached the fence and laid his hand on the top of it just beside where I was perched; then he stood a moment looking back to see if the stag needed further aid in getting clear.

Not much aid did he require. Balancing himself with his forefeet straddled well apart, but his hind feet still in the grip of the clove-hitch, by a few hard kicks he loosened the hitch until it dropped off, and instantly, with a savage roar, he rushed at Jimmy tail up and head down. But Jimmy vaulted lightly up beside me, and the baffled monster

vainly vented his fury below. From our vantage we mocked at the shattering blasts that came from his throat like blares from a trumpet, while his hot breath seemed to scorch our hands : unable to reach us he lowered his head and pawed the ground in impotent fury till the dust and dirt rained back in showers both on himself and on the mockers above.

" He'd be the boy to clear the plaza at a Mexican bullfight," cried Charley, who was squatted up on the top rail of the fence on the other side, and with that he dropped monkey-like to the ground inside the corral, waving in his hand an old gunny sack " para llamar el toro "—" to call the bull "— as the Spanish phrase has it.

" Oh, quit your monkeying," called out Jimmy angrily. " Leave him alone to cool off." But the infuriated stag had spotted the intruder, and he went for him on the instant like a tiger.

Back flew Charley like lightning on to the top rail, turning there to mock at his pursuer as we had done. But the stag had got up steam in his charge across the corral ; as he neared the fence we saw him collect himself for a spring, then his great body rose grandly at the leap, and though he hit the top rail hard with both hind legs he alighted fair and square on his feet on the outside.

" Look out for your horses ! " yelled Jimmy, springing to the ground, also on the outside, and starting for the buckskin pony, who was standing in the open.

Alas, the big yellow stag had started for him

too ! Burning to wreak his vengeance on something, he chose for his victim the horse rather
than the man. I saw Jimmy's hand go down
to his belt for the ready revolver, but even as he
did so those awful horns were thrust half a yard
into the body of the buckskin pony, and, with
one mighty heave, the great stag flung him over
his back ten feet into the air. The death-stricken
horse screamed as the horns went in : the life was
out of him, I hope, before he hit the ground.

The stag whirled round with his head aloft,
and, still breathing slaughter, looked for another
victim. Jimmy Murray was within five yards of
him with levelled pistol.

Crack ! a jet of smoke burst from the muzzle ;
the knees of the stag bent suddenly under him ;
then the solid earth shook with the thud of his
fall as he dropped in his tracks and lay kicking
convulsively. The ball had taken him in the butt
of the ear and found the brain.

Out flashed Jimmy's long, gleaming knife, and,
catching hold of one of those red-dyed horns in
his left hand, he stooped and drove the double-
edged point deep into the base of the throat. Swiftly
he rose again and planted his left foot on the heaving flank of the carcass and stood erect, aiding,
with regular rhythmical pushes, the pulses of the
streaming blood as it pumped itself from the heart
through the severed arteries.

Charley came up to mumble some apology for
having unwittingly brought about the death of
the buckskin pony.

"Can't be helped," said Jimmy grimly. "No use now to cry over spilt blood. You run over to the waggon and tell the cook to make a roaring fire and get out the spits. We'll have a real old-time barbecue to-night before we hit the trail for Texas in the morning." And that was the end of the big yellow stag, but the buckskin pony never saw Texas again.

The morning did not quite absolutely see them hitting the trail for Texas as Jimmy had hoped because the branded herd had to be moved to Big Horse Creek and turned loose there at Holt's new ranch; still, a couple more days did indeed see them off. And longingly did my thoughts turn in the same direction: here was I now being crowded out with my small TH herd in this new Colorado, where men no longer counted their droves of cattle by hundreds but by thousands and many thousands. I talked it all over with Gus and Vicente, and in the end I decided to sell out here, join in with them as partners, and take some waggon-loads of trade goods down to New Mexico, where we would see if we could not trade the goods off for sheep enough to make a very profitable drive with them back to Colorado. Mexican sheep were only about half the price of American sheep, but they were much more active and hardy, and when crossed with good rams the half-breeds produced plenty of good wool. The cross succeeded every bit as well as the cross of Texas and American cattle.

My scheme went swimmingly. I found a purchaser for the ranch, and I sold out the TH brand

to the Wilsons, not the big cattlemen of that name but another pair of Wilsons. They were right good men too, and I fixed things through the bank so as to leave a lot of the purchase money to be paid over later, but left it on good enough security to satisfy my friendly advisers.

Then I and my Mexican partners bought our goods—Gus and Vicente knew what would be suitable for trade down in New Mexico; we loaded them into a couple of waggons, fixed ourselves up as well as we knew how, and away we went. New Mexico was even wilder and woollier than Colorado in those days, and our adventures there were not a few. The tale of them I may, perhaps, tell in another story.

THE END

Timberline Books

Stephen J. Leonard and Thomas J. Noel, editors

Colorado's Japanese Americans, Bill Hosokawa

Denver: An Archaeological History, Sarah M. Nelson,
K. Lynn Berry, Richard F. Carrillo, Bonnie L. Clark,
Lori E. Rhodes, and Dean Saitta

A Tenderfoot in Colorado, R. B. Townshend

A Tenderfoot
in Colorado